AF321616

Globalization after the Pandemic

Qin Hui is one of the most original thinkers and commentators active in China today. He has long courted controversy across the political spectrum by arguing that China's development model, based on a "low human rights advantage," lacks both economic and political freedoms as well as social protection. In this wide-ranging and meticulously researched book he argues that the COVID-19 pandemic reveals decisive weaknesses in both the Chinese and European/American political systems.

While China early on chose to "control the whistleblowers" rather than the virus, Qin provocatively asks whether liberal democracies sometimes prioritized "freedom over survival." If they do not want to lose the global battle against authoritarian states, he argues, democracies should adjust their response, just as China should turn away from high-tech authoritarianism and return to the path of protecting human rights.

While not everyone will agree with Qin's conclusions, the rigor of his arguments, the broad historical and geographical range of his examples, and his commitment to defending human dignity around the world make for a compelling read and challenge all forms of pandemic complacency.

Sebastian Veg

School of Advanced Studies in the Social Sciences (EHESS), Paris

GLOBALIZATION AFTER THE PANDEMIC

Qin Hui

Translated by
David Ownby

The Chinese University of Hong Kong Press

Edges Series

Globalization after the Pandemic
    By Qin Hui
    Translated by David Ownby

ISBN: 978-988-237-231-3

The Chinese University of Hong Kong Press
The Chinese University of Hong Kong
Sha Tin, N.T., Hong Kong
Fax: +852 2603 7355
Email: cup@cuhk.edu.hk
Website: cup.cuhk.edu.hk

Printed in Hong Kong

CONTENTS

FOREWORD

BY DAVID OWNBY

In the winter and spring of 2020, when the coronavirus erupted in China and then spread around the world, I had already been studying the world of contemporary Chinese establishment intellectuals for some time, mainly by translating and "curating" important examples of their work and sharing them via my website "Reading the China Dream,"[1] as well as in print form.[2] Why are Chinese establishment intellectuals interesting? Because China's rise to superpower status, together with the West's seeming "decline" in the first decade of the 21st century, has convinced many of these intellectuals that world history is at a turning point as important as the moment when, for example, monarchies were replaced by democracies. Their reasoning is that both Soviet communism and American (or more broadly, Western) liberal democracy have failed economically and politically, while China surges forward. This means not only that China is the "wave of the future," but also that China's (and the world's) past, present, and future must be revisited, since most people's basic vision of the world has been fundamentally shaped either by liberalism—which focuses on the individual and market forces—or socialism—which focuses on class struggle and the dialectic.

The belief that liberalism and socialism have both lost their explanatory value can be liberating (it is what motivates many postmodernists, after all), and between roughly 2000 and 2015, the world of Chinese establishment intellectuals exploded in a burst of creativity not seen since the Republican Period (1912–1949) as they sought to rethink the world and China's place in it, to reimagine contemporary China's founding myths. We are of course free to agree or disagree with Chinese establishment intellectuals, but as the world's second largest economy and chief competitor with the United States, it behooves us to at least know what they are thinking, because while these figures are not dissidents, they are not propagandists either, as the book translated here richly illustrates.

The events of the spring and summer of 2020, when China largely bested the virus and the West did not, seemed in the eyes of many Chinese establishment intellectuals to confirm their view that China was rising and the West declining. I decided that Chinese intellectual commentary on the coronavirus and its management would likely become an important aspect of the broader ongoing discussion in China, and launched a project to attempt to follow along.[3] The commentary sounded some fairly predictable notes—such as a certain amount of chest-thumping pride in China's, and East Asia's, "communitarian" culture, which made collective efforts to fight the virus less onerous than in the "individualistic" West[4]—as well as exploring more interesting nooks and crannies regarding particular aspects of Chinese society and politics.[5] The project also yielded the book translated here: by far the most interesting and surprising example of anything I read by Chinese establishment intellectuals talking about the coronavirus.

In this book, Qin Hui, one of China's most prominent liberal intellectuals and champions of human rights and democracy, who often publishes, in China, things that look to me very much like "dissent," says essentially: it is a *fact* that China's authoritarian regime, through a combination of coercion and science, did a *much better job* than any major Western country in handling the pandemic, a fact which is destined to make China more powerful and more authoritarian. What are the supporters of democracy and human rights going to do about that? To drive the point home, Qin notes that if any country—or terrorist organization—ever "weaponizes" something like the coronavirus and deploys it in a war, it is clear which side will win. Again, what are the supporters of democracy and human rights going to do about that?

The Life and Work of Qin Hui

Of course, not everyone knows who Qin Hui is.[6]

Born in 1953, Qin was starting middle school in Nanning, the capital of the Guangxi Zhuang Autonomous Region, when China's Cultural Revolution began in 1966 and schools were closed so that Red Guards could make revolution. Qin joined a Red Guard faction that "dared to rebel," an experience that gave him some of his first lessons in political hypocrisy; the distance between the political slogans—those of the Red Guards and those of the government—and the reigning social reality provided much food for thought. In addition, luck had it that Qin had joined the losing side in a fight with huge personal consequences: he spent nine years—between the ages of fifteen and twenty-four—as a sent-down youth[7] in a mountainous remote Zhuang (a minority ethnicity in China) village on the border between Guangxi and Yunnan. Both the remoteness of the village and the length of Qin's stay were conditioned by Qin's early political *faux pas*. Qin nonetheless joined the Chinese Communist Party, of his own volition, during his stint in the countryside.

In 1978, when China's universities reopened, Qin managed to gain entry to an MA program in History, having skipped over middle school, high school, and university. Clearly, Qin had used his "free time" in the village to educate himself, even learning English, testimony to his great intelligence and energy, as well as the lack of much else meaningful to do. He studied in Lanzhou, in northwest China, in order to work with Professor Zhao Lisheng (1917–2007), a well-known specialist in the history of rural China, who at the time focused on topics such as peasant wars and landlord exploitation. Qin worked diligently on these subjects for at least a dozen years before enlarging his field of study, but the questions he asked and the answers at which he arrived continue to guide Qin's work even today.

To make a long story short, Qin ultimately decided to abandon the classic approach to rural studies, an approach grounded in Marxist theory, and to replace it with a more empirical methodology, based in textual documentation or facts gathered through fieldwork. His research led him to reject the Marxist vision, which saw rural conflicts as the product of a class struggle between peasants and landlords; Qin's interpretation was that these conflicts were the result of abuses perpetrated by an authoritarian state, in the form of arbitrary taxes, the appropriation of peasant property, or excessive corvée labor exactions. Qin's work, carried out at first with his professor and later with his wife, Jin Yan, a well-known specialist of the history of Russia and Eastern Europe, has both historical and comparative dimensions, and is impressive in its sophistication and complexity. His research also has implications for contemporary politics; the People's Communes established during the Great Leap Forward in 1957 had been abandoned in the early 1980s. The problem of China's rural order—or more broadly, the question of the treatment of China's rural population—thus emerged once again in the Reform and Opening period and in many senses still awaits a solution.

Qin Hui lost his faith in communism—or at least communism as it is practiced in China—when Deng Xiaoping sent troops to fire on student demonstrators in Tiananmen Square in 1989. Subsequently, his research became more polemical if not necessarily more political, but he has never abandoned his primary identity as someone who does serious professional research, and most of his publications over the course of the 1990s continued to focus on typically academic subjects. At the end of the 1990s, however, we begin to note the publication of works like *The Market Yesterday and Today: Consumer Society, the Rationality of the Market, and Social Justice*,[8] where Qin's research questions take on more abstract, general dimensions, or *The Farmers Speak: Collected Essays on Peasant Studies*,[9] where Qin traces his own intellectual evolution through the presentation of already published essays. The same year (1999) he published *Problems and "Isms,"*[10] taking up a trope from the New Culture Movement of the 1920s to criticize his colleagues who lose themselves in "theory" without paying attention to the social reality around them.

Similar works followed. In 2003, Qin published *Ten Thesis on Tradition*,[11] which aimed to revisit received wisdom on the "Chinese tradition," and *Peasant China: Historical Reflections and Contemporary Choices*,[12] which is a variation on the same theme. The following year, Qin published *Practice and Freedom*,[13] which looks at the exchanges between the state and the peasants in the context of changes in China's rural order. In 2007, he published *The Path of Reform*,[14] which enlarged on Qin's opinions on the subject, emphasizing among other things the importance of human rights (especially, but not solely, in China's rural context). In 2013, Qin published *South African Perspectives*,[15] an important part of which is a long treatment of "China as Seen from South Africa," where Qin compares the treatment of Black South Africans and Chinese migrant laborers in terms of the roles both have played in the economic development of their respective countries, as well as the treatment they have received at the hands of those countries. Qin finds that the roles the two played were similar, in the sense that both states took advantage of cheap labor created by artificial status barriers (the system of racial discrimination in South Africa, the internal passport—*hukou*—system in China). Qin also argues that, in general, South African Blacks have been treated better than Chinese migrant workers.

It is not easy to sum up Qin Hui's *oeuvre*. Isaiah Berlin grouped writers and thinkers in two categories: hedgehogs and foxes. The hedgehog (Plato) knows one thing, but it's a big and fundamental thing. The fox (Shakespeare) knows many things. Qin Hui (who could be the Chinese Isaiah Berlin if such a thing were possible) is both hedgehog and fox.

I've explored Qin's "fox" side a bit in the preceding paragraphs. As for his "hedgehog" side, the fundamental thing that Qin has understood, and which guides him in practically all of his research work, is the idea that ideology—any ideology—exists to obscure the ways in which authorities abuse their power. He works at two levels. First, he illustrates the flawed reality on the ground, and then he proceeds to try to take apart the ideology that has constructed and defends the flawed reality. As a result, his only allegiance is to the fundamental rights of humanity and, by implication, to the constitutions that defend those rights. But he is profoundly distrustful of *any* political or ideological *system*, because all systems, be they "democratic," "socialist," or "authoritarian," are grounded in power, and power inevitably results in abuse. In many instances, Qin even seems mistrustful of stylistic elegance, less for "ideological" reasons and more because style can be a mask that camouflages the truth just as ideology can be an apology for abuses of power, telling us a story in order to sell us on reality as it exists.

An excellent example of this is his 2015 text on "Dilemmas of Twenty-First Century Globalization," in which, enlarging on his self-appointed task to review Thomas Piketty's work, *Twenty-First Century Capitalism*, Qin offers his own reading of the destinies of "capitalism" and "socialism" in the age of globalization.[16]

Piketty focuses on the problem of increasing economic inequality in all developed economies, and compiles massive data sets illustrating that, with very few exceptions, capital is systematically invested in financial instruments rather than in the productive economy. This fundamental characteristic of capitalism means that inequality is a natural result of market function, and that the fight against inequality, which handicaps more and more the workings of the capitalist system in developed countries, requires active state intervention to assure the necessary redistribution.

Qin Hui rejects Piketty's analysis, as well as the debate that Piketty's work inspired. In Qin's view, the source of the inequalities that are plaguing the developed economies is China, which has taken advantage of the workings of globalization to erode the very foundation of Western prosperity in the post-War period. His basic argument is simple: when China rejoined the world economy in the Reform and Opening period, capital from throughout the world rushed to China to take advantage of China's cheap labor and what Qin calls China's "low human rights advantage"—in other words, the Chinese state's willingness to pursue economic development at any price, including land confiscation, the suppression of workers' rights, and the exploitation of migrant labor, among other things (that the Chinese state has been doing long before becoming communist). Over time, China became the "factory of the world," producing quality items at cheap prices, to the detriment of jobs and tax receipts in what until then had been the developed world, now abandoned by capital, which preferred the Chinese El Dorado. Despite a surplus of capital and increasingly frequent labor shortages, the power of the Chinese state keeps the machine churning, loaning Chinese profits back to developed economies so that the "exchange" can continue. The debts created in this way only intensify the crisis of the developed world, because these governments attempt in any event to deliver more "welfare" to a growing number of unemployed despite the fall in tax revenues.

Thus, according to Qin, Piketty misses the point, first because no state can "redistribute" money that does not exist, and second, because the debate provoked by Piketty's book was all about different capitalist "models" (American, European, Scandinavian), while in fact all of these economies are in the same boat when it comes to China. As a result, not only is there no conflict between "capitalism" and "socialism"—all developed economies being a mixture of the two and China being a free-rider—but ideology blinds the developed world to what is actually happening: the abuse of the world system by the Chinese state. Consistent with arguments he has made elsewhere, Qin demands that Chinese workers receive the same rights as better-protected workers elsewhere. Thanks to Qin's research, we see here the immemorial conflict between the peasants and the Chinese state transposed onto the globalized economy of the 21st century.

Qin explores this "immemorial conflict between the peasants and the Chinese state" in his 2015 (banned) book, *Abandoning the Imperial System*.[17] The book offers a new reading of a key period between the fall of the Qing in 1911 and the establishment of the Communist regime in 1949, generally known as China's Republican Period, because a republican regime replaced the dynasty, to be replaced in turn by the People's Republic. I mentioned above the effort by Chinese establishment intellectuals to "reimagine China" and to create "new founding myths" for China's contemporary experience, a challenge inspired by China's rise in the early 21st century. The period examined by Qin in his book is *the* crucial period for those attempting to rethink China, because all of the central elements in any narrative of modern China's history are found here: the failure of the dynastic order, the establishment of the Republic, the May Fourth Movement, the establishment of the Chinese Communist Party, the Nanjing Decade, the anti-Japanese War, and the Communist victory in 1949.

Qin's book is in fact a reaction *against* a conservative, New Confucian rereading of this entire period, which insists that both the "democratic" choices (especially those of the May Fourth Movement), as well as the "socialist" choices were all unfortunate and erroneous, because they were not *"Chinese"* choices. This rereading, in which the late-Qing reformer Kang Youwei (1858–1927) plays a major role as the principal Confucian "hero," argues that despite important conflicts with the West, China was, at the moment of the Revolution of 1911, well on its way toward the establishment of a constitutional monarchy, the achievement of which would have allowed China to avoid a painful rupture with its glorious tradition, as well as a century of violent and unnecessary revolution(s).

Qin rejects this argument completely. According to Qin, the Revolution of 1911 was neither unnecessary nor a failure, because it put an end to the imperial regime, what he calls the "Qin system," a regime that had defined the entire dynastic history of China. Far from being "Confucian" as widely asserted, the spirit of this regime was instead "Legalist," a philosophy championed by Qin Shi Huang (259–210 BCE), China's first emperor, and which attempted to concentrate all power in the hands of the emperor at the expense of the rights of the people. This system, vestiges of which continue to exist today, abuses its power without assuming its responsibilities to the people. The fall of the Qin system occurred when the Chinese people, and above all the Chinese elite, understood that Western, constitutional systems were stronger, more efficient, *and* more virtuous than the Qin system. In light of this, the arguments of today's New Confucians that the Revolution of 1911 was unnecessary do not hold water. The Revolution of 1911 was imperative, and its promise is yet to be realized, because China's regime is not fully constitutional.

The Coronavirus and Globalization

Finally we arrive at Qin's book on the pandemic and globalization. To my knowledge, this text has not been published in China or in Chinese, or at least searching the title on internet does not lead me to a link. Over the course of the spring of 2020, I noted an online announcement that Qin was going to give a public lecture of the topic, and wrote him asking if he had a draft I could read. My memory is that the talk was cancelled, but there is a YouTube recording[18] (without images) of a talk with the same name from some time in April, so perhaps not. In any event, Qin emailed me his text on October 16, 2020, asking me to translate it, and it appears here in book form for the first time. In the current climate in China, it may not be possible to publish a probing, critical treatment of a sensitive topic.

Qin's text is a stunning reflection on the successes and failures of fighting the coronavirus in China and the rest of the world, but his principal focus is on China and the West. As always, his goal is to cut through the rhetoric, the finger-pointing, and the chest-thumping to get to the simple, if chilling, crux of the issue: China used its "low human rights advantage" to impose coercive lockdowns that rapidly got the virus under control after the disastrous outbreak in Wuhan, while the West, handicapped by its "high human rights (dis)advantage," stumbled badly, and continues to stumble. Yet the point of Qin's text is not to sing China's praises, but instead to wake the West up to the flaws in its institutions revealed by the failure to get the virus under control, the sad fact that Western concern with human rights has—understandably if tragically—increased the number of cases of illness and death. As mentioned above, Qin asks us to imagine the scenario in which the conspiracy theories asserting that the coronavirus had been engineered by a Chinese laboratory or by the American military were to come true, and the world found itself in a state of biological warfare using contagions vastly more lethal than the current virus. What are the chances that Western democracies would win? Or even survive?

Qin very much wants democracy to survive and prosper, in the West and eventually in China as well. His text is thus an even-handed and objective criticism *of both China and the West,* a rare bird in such polarized times. His criticisms of China are fairly straightforward. Allow freedom of speech and leave whistle-blowers alone, which would have expedited the management of the initial crisis in Wuhan and perhaps spared the rest of the China—and the rest of the world—the pain and loss of the subsequent pandemic. Stop bragging about China's superior performance in fighting the virus. The "medieval" methods China used were not invented in China but came from the West, and the reason for China's success was their "low human rights advantage," which facilitated the imposition of coercive measures. Be vigilant that the heightened powers seized by the state during the emergency not become permanent additions to what is already a potent arsenal.

Qin's criticisms of the West are more complex and indeed often difficult to follow. This makes sense because here we have a Chinese champion of democracy and human rights essentially telling the West that human rights concerns have blinded them to the greater importance of human life during an emergency. Clearly exasperated by those who claim the human right "not to wear a mask" (as well as by their opponents who refuse to recognize that they indeed have this "right," even if exercising it in the moment is inappropriate), Qin offers a long disquisition on the confusion that occurs when we conflate rights with values.

A right, Qin insists, is the ability to do, or not to do, a certain thing, and hence equivalent to a freedom. Such rights are not absolute (you cannot scream "fire" in a crowded theater because you have freedom or speech), nor is the exercise of a right always a good thing (I have the right to tell my boss exactly what I think of him, or to pick my nose on a first date). The right to bear arms is treated as God-given and absolute in the United States, but not even the NRA defends the right to bear *nuclear* arms. Some rights—such as the right to smoke cigarettes or market opioids— have serious consequences for public health. Some rights—such as the right to whistle on a crowded bus—are simply stupid (and yet not easily taken away).

If we stop and think about it, it is immediately obvious that "give me liberty or give me death," however inspiring, in no way describes how we live our daily lives (we wait in line, we take turns), to say nothing of the calculations necessary in times of emergency. Qin Hui has spent much of his life writing about the fundamental importance of human rights, and it clearly pains him to say to the West that "rights discourse has gotten out of hand." But he says it, and without attacking "political correctness," as are many of his fellow liberals in China. Rights, Qin insists, are one element of community and political life, and should not absolutized or decontextualized.

Next, Qin tackles the related question of dictatorship, reminding Westerners that historically, the first dictators were Roman military figures who received a special and temporary mandate in times of war, when democracy was suspended. In other words, this institution is part of the West's heritage, even if in modern times it has been associated with the scourge of communism and thus seen as the antithesis of democracy, instead of a temporary interruption (Qin notes for good measure that Lenin's—and China's—"democratic dictatorship" makes no sense in historical or logical terms). Qin is clearly aware that democracy has indeed been "interrupted" during wartime more than once in modern history, but is frustrated by the hesitation of Western democratic leaders to use the powers at their disposal to fight a different sort of "war." (Qin being Qin, we also have several paragraphs on the differences between waging war against a declared enemy and fighting a non-human virus.)

There is much, much more to the essay: the rise and fall of serfdom after the Black Death (which followed a similar logic to the growth of China's economy under conditions of global-ization); revelations concerning little-known pandemics that occurred in the People's Republic; the invention of the practice of quarantine in medieval Venice; the history of leprosy; the Siracusa principles, established in 1984, which attempt to establish how to deal with human rights under states of emergency. The text is long and fascinating, if at times a bit obscure, in part because Qin often returns to arguments developed in other contexts without informing the reader, in part perhaps because he does not want to be *too* clear in certain criticisms that may be addressed to China's over-sensitive premier leader. But to my mind, the best way to view the length and difficulty of the text is to see it as a reflection of the difficulty of the question Qin is trying to answer: How do we save democracy when one part of the organism—rights discourse—has metastasized out of control, endangering the survival of the organism itself?

CHAPTER ONE

What if "Human Rights" Means "No Humans Left"?[*]

The great coronavirus pandemic that erupted in the winter of 2019 has finally calmed down in China, after the bungling occasioned by the silencing of the whistle-blowers, the iron hand of the lockdown, certain changes in the virus itself, and the painful price paid by the Chinese people, particularly the Chinese people of Wuhan—although the epidemic could of course return. But beginning in March 2020, the disaster spread abroad, and at present there is no end in sight.

Discussions of the changes the pandemic will bring to China and the world, together with stories from the past about how "plagues changed history," are a hot topic everywhere. Given the recent world situation, most of the discussion has followed the rubric of the rise and fall of great powers, with everyone happily talking about who is at risk in the post-pandemic world, and who stands to gain, and what the new international order will be, and whether there will be a new "number one." Which leads to discussion of the "civilizational change" linked to the influence of economic culture tied to these historical musings. We await the pundit's pronouncements.

My goal in this book is to discuss one central theme: the impact of the pandemic on institutions. From the point of view of the history of mankind, the rise and fall of the great powers is a blip on the radar screen; the fate of institutions is much more important to our common destiny. Over the past century and a half, the world's most powerful nation has changed from the United Kingdom to the United States, which was really no big deal. As the Qing-period Chinese novel *Unofficial History of the Scholars* puts it, "the river flows to the east for thirty years, and then to the west for thirty years," so it is simply a question of changes in the wind and the water. If the change had been from Britain to Nazi Germany, then it would have been dangerous, because in that case it would not have been a simple question of who is number one and who is number two, but instead a question of civilization and barbarism for the whole human race.

From the perspective of history, certain plagues have brought about institutional changes, but, as I have stressed many times before, while the standard of human progress may be universal, specific historical processes are inherently uncertain. The "cause" of a plague and the "outcome" it brings may be different, or even the complete opposite, depending on certain conditions. The famous example of the Black Death and the rise and fall of serfdom in the late Middle Ages is one example.

Globalization and the Rise and Fall of Serfdom after the Black Death

In Western Europe, one of the most significant consequences of the Black Death was that it caused or at least hastened the disappearance of serfdom. Prior to the plague, serfdom in Western Europe was already showing signs of decline. After the plague, population declined, land was abundant, and labor was in short supply. This, coupled with the fact that death and depopulation were more severe in the cities than in the countryside—due to the high population density and contagion rate of the epidemic—plus the fact that there were more urban employment opportunities during the recovery period, led peasants to migrate to the cities. Under these circumstances, feudal lords competed for labor and were forced to offer better terms to peasants, reducing feudal obligations, improving their legal status and income, removing physical constraints, and encouraging farmers in their territories to start families and increase the population. Some lords even changed their economic strategy, moving from labor-intensive agriculture to capital-intensive sheep farming, abandoning serfdom and contracting out land to tenants. As a result, serfdom died away in Western Europe, especially in England.[1] And free peasants, whether they were initially tenant farmers or hired laborers, benefited from rising wages due to the scarcity of land and falling land rents.[2] The freeing of the serfs and the increase in the incomes of free farmers led to the flourishing of family farms, the so-called late medieval "agricultural revolution" in Western Europe, and to a boom in handicrafts, commodity economy, cities, as well as the rise of civil society.

Of course, it was not necessarily smooth sailing for Western Europe from that point forward. There were still bumps in the road between the era of the Black Death and the pre-modernization period, and no one would "attribute" moderization entirely to the terrible plague. However, most scholars today who look at history from the perspective of the *longue durée* acknowledge that the changes that occurred in Western Europe after the Black Death, especially the elimination of serfdom, played a huge role in the modernization of the region, which was the first to emerge from the Middle Ages.

We know that the unprecedented bubonic plague entered Europe from the Middle East and then swept across almost all of Europe from southwest to northeast, skipping a few "islands," such as southeastern Poland and Milan, Italy. But in the Middle East, the source of the infection of Western and Southern Europe, and in Eastern Europe, which was infected by Southwestern Europe, the social changes following the Black Death were the exact opposite of those in Western Europe: serfdom in the Middle East remained intact, while in Eastern Europe, where serfdom had not previously existed, the practice became increasingly widespread, even replacing free small farmers in the centuries following the Black Death, in what was called "late-developing serfdom" or the "second edition of serfdom" in Eastern Europe. In the context of Europe as a whole, it is also known as the "second serfdom" (Western European serfdom being the first).

What is interesting is that this strengthening of serfdom in Eastern Europe and the Middle East has been attributed to the same factors that led to the disappearance of serfdom in Western

Europe: the scarcity of people and the abundance of land in the aftermath of the plague that created a labor shortage. E. D. Domar (1914–1997), the prominent Russian-American economic historian, argued that because of the scarcity of labor, feudal masters, fearing that the peasants would flee, bound them more tightly to the land, turning free peasants into serfs. Under conditions of labor surplus, there are always many fish in the sea, and there is no need to bind the peasants to the land.[3] This is known as the Domar Theory of the relationship between abundant land, population scarcity, and feudalism.[4] This theory seems to be confirmed by the fact that in China, in the chaos following the fall of the Han dynasty, the population declined drastically, and forms of serfdom such as *buqu* 部曲 and *sishu* 私屬[5] were prevalent.

Why did the Black Death, which led to depopulation in both regions, cause the demise of serfdom in Western Europe and the rise of serfdom in Eastern Europe and the Middle East? From a purely economic perspective, people holding things in short supply should be in a better bargaining position than people holding things that are in surplus. Thus it was logical that labor scarcity should have favored the worker. But this only works under conditions of competition. In Western Europe, the feudal lords competed for scarce manpower by offering advantages to the peasants in the form of lower rents, higher wages, freedom, and so on. But as a young scholar at Stanford recently pointed out, the feudal lords of the Middle East and Eastern Europe were able to avoid such competition, because the period following the Black Death saw the rise of centralized, authoritarian empires: the Turkish Ottoman Empire and the Russian Tsarist Empire. These empires obviated the need for competition among the nobility to recruit serfs, because the monarchy could simply allocate serfs to the nobles and help them capture runaways, so the feudal masters did not have to "sweet-talk" the peasants in order to hire them. Instead, sweet-talking the emperor was a better way for feudal lords to obtain even more serfs, and their "allocation" required that their status be changed from peasant to serf, for which the emperor's power was useful. Given these conditions, it would have been a wonder if serfdom had *not* flourished. [6]

At the time he articulated his theory, Domar did not consider these political factors. However, he did mention another economic factor, in addition to the scarcity of labor, which stimulated the development of serfdom in Eastern Europe: after the demise of serfdom in Western Europe, a market economy and civil society began to emerge, and economic development and consumption levels surged ahead of those of Eastern Europe. The demand in Western Europe for agricultural products, whether as direct consumer goods or as industrial raw materials, increased greatly as a result, leading to the emergence of a thriving export-oriented agriculture in land-rich, sparsely populated Eastern Europe. In this context, small, self-sufficient, free farmers were indeed inferior to feudal estates in terms of productivity. Relying on its "low human rights advantage," the Russian manor economy, which exported grain to Western Europe, had its beginnings in the 16th century and reached its peak in the 18th century after the Industrial Revolution in Western Europe. The export capacity of the feudal estates made the Russian economy the model of a high surplus economy among the major powers of the time, and the Russian Empire, which had absorbed large agricultural areas such as Poland and Ukraine, became the "breadbasket of Europe" and indeed one of the breadbaskets of the world, just as China has become the "factory of the world" over the past few decades. Western Europe, advanced and free, was running a trade deficit and exporting capital to the late-developing but rapidly growing feudal Russian empire, which might be seen as one of the first signs of globalization and its contradictions.

Political Institutions and Epidemiology

Today's coronavirus is certainly not the same thing as the medieval Black Death. But in terms of their impact on humanity's institutions, we can identify parallels between the two.

The first period of the epidemic played out mainly in China, and the second period moved abroad, especially to Europe and the United States. Both periods have produced a certain number of "maxims." Regarding China, we have:

"They started by shutting down the whistle-blowers, which led to locking down the city."

"Without the shameless 404," (the Internet code for "page not found") "there would be no lamentations on April 4" (the date on which Wuhan's collective Qingming funeral was held).[7]

"They shut down a few whistles and the mourning flutes blew sadly throughout the country" (another reference to Qingming).

"First they hid little things that became large things, and then they concentrated their forces to take care of the big things."

And finally, "The system first shat on the world, then showed the world how good it was at wiping its ass."

The maxims about Europe and America were even funnier: "Quarantine, no human rights; no quarantine, no humans left."[8]

Then there's the Chinese-English pun: "Quarantine, I see you, no quarantine, ICU!"

And this one comments on both China and the West: "China's way of fighting the pandemic relied on two factors: the first is that the people are really obedient, and the second is that they are really afraid of dying; the outbreak of the pandemic in Europe and the United States also relied on two factors: the first is that the people are really disobedient, and the second is that they are really not afraid of dying."

Whether or not they are accurate, these maxims touch on institutional questions that are worth thinking about. The facts of the epidemic in both China and the West show that it is not appropriate to shut down the whistle-blowers, but also that this is not adequate in and of itself. The Western experience illustrates that not shutting down whistle-blowers does not cause panic, which means that it was unreasonable for China to use the prevention of panic as a reason for doing so. But the absence of panic does not in itself prevent epidemics. Suppressing the whistle-blowers indeed spread the coronavirus in China, but when that spread is a *fait accompli*, it doesn't really matter what you do with whistle-blowers—it matters whether you can effectively lock down a city.

Of course, some commentators are also avoiding institutional issues, in two typical ways. One is through conspiracy theories, which blame the whole thing either on China's plotting to bring down the United States or the United States' plotting to bring down China, i.e., the old story of "the gang leader fighting with his rival." The other is the "culture theory," which says that Chinese culture is able to accept mask-wearing and isolation, while Westerners experience "cultural resistance" to mask-wearing and isolation. There are two possible motives behind this latter argument: some Chinese are bursting with "cultural confidence"[9] and believe that Chinese culture is superior in all ways to Western culture. Others are trying to avoid the awkward dilemma posed by the way in which the existing democratic institutions in the West have dealt with the pandemic, and prefer instead to talk about "culture."

In fact, it is true that in both China and in the West, the average person rarely likes to wear a mask under normal conditions, and it is also true that people's perceptions differ when faced with a serious threat. Yet there are only two differences that count: first, how much institutional pressure is exerted to make the wearing of masks compulsory? Obviously, China exerted more pressure. Second, even if you are willing to wear a mask, can you get one? In fact, during the first phase of the pandemic, which occurred in China, China consumed most of the world's masks, and many European and American cities had none to sell, so that even if many people were willing to wear a mask, there were none to wear. Preventing panic buying in times of scarcity and giving priority to the infected and to health care workers instead of pressuring the general public makes sense, and this has nothing to do with the "culture of refusing to wear a mask." In fact, as I argue below, the wearing of masks and face coverings (of course in their primitive form) to prevent infection, like the dual quarantine system, may well have been pioneered by Westerners, as far as we can see.

drugs for Vietnam, but in fact it had nothing to do with Vietnam and instead with the malaria outbreak in South China. I myself experienced the epidemic and contracted malaria, and also participated in the six-year-long "anti-malaria war." In Tianlin County, Guangxi Province, where I was sent down during the Cultural Revolution, there were 1,480 malaria cases per year on average in the seventeen years prior to the Cultural Revolution, but the chaos of the period led to a malaria epidemic in 1969, with the number of cases soaring to 15,148 the following year, more than ten times greater than the previous seventeen-year average, and 14% of the population of this county, with a population of only 110,000, suffered from the disease. Of course, the subsequent "great war against malaria" also demonstrated the advantages of the Chinese "national system," but it was 1983—the beginning of the Reform and Opening period—before the incidence rate was brought back to the pre-Cultural Revolution level.[12]

In the current coronavirus epidemic, the mistakes made by the Chinese system in the early days were also serious and go far beyond "admonishing" a few "whistle-blowers," nor can they be explained away as due to a "lack of awareness of a new disease" or as necessary "to prevent panic." Leaving aside the controversial Fang Fang's *Wuhan Diary*[13] and other people disliked by the authorities, Professor Hua Sheng (b. 1953) is clearly a prominent academic, close to the government, whose series of studies in the early days of the coronavirus epidemic have been accused by some of having been a case of "lending a hand" to China's top authorities who were scrambling to save face, a claim that the authorities have hardly bothered to refute. A netizen on the popular Chinese discussion site Zhihu commented: "Many voices have been suppressed, but one person is speaking out very 'boldly,' which is absurd in itself."[14] This represents the thoughts of many of those skeptical of Prof. Hua Sheng.

But Hua Sheng's accusations give one pause:

> Wuhan City's series of deliberately designed traps…did not hesitate to use all kinds of serious violations of law and discipline… to cover up the truth, suppress and crack down on doctors and insiders who told the truth…Having amassed mighty powers, they [city officials] ignore Party discipline and the laws of the country, ignore the people's health and livelihood, believing that punishing people is normal and that running roughshod over them is the same as competence. As long as they can maintain their glamorous appearance and powerful position, once they have grasped power, they will issue commands left and right, stopping at nothing to deceive their superiors and hiding things from the people, ignoring all legal and moral principles.[15]

As commentators said, these words "cut to the quick," and their revelations about high officials (though only in Hubei and Wuhan) are more revealing than what pro-government Internet trolls called the "traitorous remarks" of Fang Fang's diaries. In fact, Fang Fang only wrote about the misery of the people at the grassroots, and did not openly take stabs at high officials. As has already been pointed out on the Internet, if what Hua Sheng says is true, then those high officials should not simply be removed from their posts but imprisoned as criminals or even executed for evasion of responsibility. And whether or not Wuhan officials are completely responsible for the matter, their responsibility is extremely heavy.[16]

Think about it. Is this kind of crime imaginable in a democratic country? The fight of United States against the pandemic has been a disaster, and Trump has taken a drubbing in public opinion. But what are they accusing him of? Simply that he only cares about his re-election, that his measures against the pandemic are too sloppy and lax, too "Zen" (*Foxi* 佛系)[17], and that his idea to get back to work while the pandemic is still in course is too risky. As for his re-election, we all know that in countries like the United States, this requires doing your utmost to please the largest number of voters, which is synonymous with following "popular opinion." Can a sloppy attempt to fight the pandemic truly please the people? If not, what does this do to the argument that Trump is only thinking about his re-election? If it does please them, it can only mean the American people have themselves taken the road to ruin. In that case, those who oppose democracy can indeed say that the people are ignorant and unworthy to rule, and that His Majesty should make up his own precious mind without bothering about the voters. But this is not a criticism of Trump, and instead a criticism of democracy. The anti-Trump people are mostly Democrats; is this what they are saying?

I personally detest Trump, and give him very poor marks for much of what he does, including his policies to fight the pandemic. However, it seems that no one in the United States would accuse Trump of "a series of deliberately designed traps," of "covering up the truth, suppressing and cracking down on doctors and insiders who told the truth," and "having grasped power, stopping at nothing to deceive their superiors and hiding things from the people." Data on the pandemic in the United States is independently collected, compiled, and published by a fully autonomous, private, purely academic institution—Johns Hopkins University. Neither Trump, nor the government, nor the Congress can interfere, so can he really "cover up the truth"?

It is well known that Trump hates the American media, but his spats with the media are at worst unseemly. What publication has he shut down, what editor has he had fired? What government office in the United States can "admonish" doctors and "suppress and crack down on those who tell the truth"? Trump has had disagreements with the Centers for Disease Control (CDC) and has shared his views with the public on television. It's true that it is improper for a president to make false statements on such professional issues, but does he have CDC and public health agencies in the palm of his hand in the way that Hua Sheng described the Wuhan officials' "series of deliberately designed traps"? Trump is crude, impulsive, with many scandals that are said to be pending investigation, and in my view, as a politician, he does not measure up. But even if the portrait of someone "having grasped power, stopping at nothing to deceive their superiors and hiding things from the people," is one that might appeal to him, in the American system it is not available to him.

Trump is certainly not blameless for the pandemic mess in the United States, but the problem is really more due to the weakness of conventional democracy in the face of things such as pandemics, and is not simply a matter of a "bad president." This is something those of us who advocate democracy must seriously face up to.

Democracy Indeed Has Weak Spots: Behind the Reversal of the Pandemic Drama

In the opening innings of the coronavirus epidemic, China suffered heavy losses, and the harsh closure of the city plunged Wuhan into misery for a time. In addition to the foreseeable costs, other events, such as the Red Cross's decision to give priority to cadres in the allocation of masks, the closure of buildings and households in such way that there was no exit, resulting in non-epidemic deaths or collateral deaths that should not have occurred, also made the disaster worse for the afflicted area.

But later on, as the coronavirus became an unstoppable global pandemic, China's success was also unquestionable. By mid-May, the first wave of the epidemic in China had basically ended, while the epidemic in Europe and the United States was spreading like wildfire. After May, China experienced two successive crises, a Russian-imported case and a local epidemic in Xinfadi, Beijing, but they were quickly brought under control by imposing strict controls. Yet in the United States and some European countries, when the epidemic seemed to weaken and work resumed, there was a resurgence in mid-June, which was clearly more serious than the mild outbreak Beijing suffered. Although China raised the number of reported deaths in Wuhan by exactly 50% in April, triggering criticism of "hidden reporting," still, compared with Europe and the United States, both the number of confirmed cases and the number of deaths told very different stories, and the gap continued to grow over the next two months.

As of June 27, 2020, China's official cumulative total was 85,151 confirmed cases and 4,648 deaths, while outside of China, the cumulative total was 4,019,768 confirmed cases and 489,423 deaths. The percentage of Chinese coronavirus deaths among all such deaths in the world had fallen from more than 90% in February to less than 1% by the end of June, and even if we take into account differences in statistical measures and data inaccuracies, or even if we increased China's numbers several times for a variety of reasons, a large difference will remain. Japan and South Korea seem to have been more successful than Europe and the United States in fighting the epidemic, but the number of confirmed cases and deaths per population are still higher than that of China. So far, the only Asian countries where the number of coronavirus confirmed cases and deaths is lower than that of mainland China—not only in absolute terms but also in terms of average population size—are Vietnam and Thailand, as well as some small underdeveloped countries and poor landlocked countries where serious statistics are hard to come by and population mobility is very low.

The overwhelming majority of the developed democracies have suffered heavy losses, even if they had to "come from behind." The epidemic in Japan and South Korea came later than in China and soon became worse (on a per capita basis); the epidemic in Western Europe came later than in Japan and South Korea and soon became worse; the epidemic in the United States came later still than in Western Europe and soon became worse; the cumulative number of confirmed cases in the United States reached 2.55 million on June 27, 2020, with 127,000 deaths. In per capita terms, this is more than in most Western European countries. the United States's population is 23% of China's, yet the cumulative number of coronavirus deaths is twenty-seven times higher than China's, and even almost 50% higher than China's cumulative number of confirmed cases. Even insisting that China is "hiding information" will not explain away a contrast this great. Of course, there are also claims that as the virus mutates, the tendency is for it to become more infectious and less virulent, possibly culminating in an intractable but low-mortality "flu"-type epidemic. This may explain the "coming from behind" phenomenon described above. This does not deny that the democracies were less effective than China in the second part of the epidemic, but it does call into question the claim that "East Asian cultures" were more effective in fighting the epidemic: Japan and South Korea suffered less than the United States, probably because they contracted the epidemic early, when the infectious power of the virus was relatively low. But their epidemic was worse than China's, which can only be attributed to the "low human rights advantage" of the Chinese system.

Among places generally recognized to have a democratic system, it would seem that only Taiwan, with a cumulative total of 447 confirmed cases and seven deaths so far (at the end of June 2020), achieved results far lower than mainland China in terms of both total and average population. This is truly miraculous and worthy of further study, but one of the factors may also be the serious deterioration of relations between Taiwan's current Democratic Progressive Party (DPP) government and the Mainland, where Mainland sanctions have led to a significant con-traction of cross-strait contacts. If an epidemic like today's had occurred when the policies of the "Three Direct Links" and "free travel" were in full bloom some years ago, one wonders whether Taiwan would have been able to pull off today's miracle. Perhaps the Mainland's sanctions turned out to be a blessing in disguise.

Counter-measures employed in democratic countries against the pandemic vary between two poles. At one extreme we find "laid-back" cases like Japan and Sweden, which rely more on conscious public prevention and control and herd immunity (natural immunity), and at the other extreme we have the examples of Italy and Spain, which rely more on official measures such as compulsory quarantines (some call these measures "iron-fisted"). Many countries have tried both, with varying degrees of control. The United Kingdom, for example, began by declaring that it would stay away from compulsory measures, and then moved to tougher controls when the epidemic grew so fast that even the Prime Minister was infected. India did the same thing in reverse, starting out with relatively strong controls, then relaxing them to allow for resumption of work due to economic pressures. The United States, on the other hand, has been alternately laid-back, and has imposed and diminished controls, and policies vary considerably from state to state in a federal system. In general, however, democratic countries generally do not accept being highly regulated, and if a more relaxed posture is at all possible, they try to regulate as little as possible. Even when they do, they are unlikely to be as forceful as China.

It has been said on the Internet that northern Italy has had "harsher" lockdowns than China during the epidemic. It is true that the parliaments of democracies may agree to draconian closure laws, but China did not stop with locking down cities. At the beginning of the epidemic, after some Chinese officials made the big mistake of "stopping at nothing to deceive their superiors and hide things from the people" and blocking information, they then jumped to the other extreme by "stopping at nothing" and forcibly locking down the city. In comparison with later lockdowns in the United States and Europe, China in fact not only locked down cities, but also locked down streets, villages, districts, apartment buildings, residential units, and even individual houses. During Xi Jinping's inspection of Wuhan in mid-March, two police officers were stationed on the balcony of each house he passed by to prevent family members from approaching his motorcade.[18] What democratic country can do this?

China's attitude towards its own expatriates and international students abroad is also unimaginable to democratic countries. At the beginning of the outbreak in China, when China locked down Wuhan and some foreign countries closed their doors to China, both China and the WHO protested this unfriendly approach. Then the epidemic reversed itself and China itself closed its doors to foreign countries even more tightly. Actually this is all normal. What country isn't afraid of an epidemic coming in? But other countries simply denied entry to foreigners, and not only recognized the right of their own citizens abroad to return, but also did what they could to help, even if they had to quarantine again when they returned home. Even at the peak of the epidemic in China, when the West was calm and had closed its doors to China, they were still actively trying to bring back their own citizens who wished to return home from China. But China doesn't play that game, and when it closes its doors to the outside world, it also locks out Chinese abroad. The ambassadors' condemnation of those wishing to return was harsh, and the penalties for violating the law and slipping back into the country merciless.[19] This is something that even those countries whose laws on locking down cities are said to be "stricter than China's" cannot do.

Of course, China's draconian controls rely not only on police and the omnipresent state "organization," but also, in unprecedented ways, on high tech. In its fight against the epidemic, China is also using mobile phones to exercise "big data" control, tracking people in an extremely invasive way. Particularly in May and June during the "small outbreaks" in Heilongjiang and Xinfadi in Beijing, some places upgraded residents' ordinary passes to a tracking health code on their smartphones, and then to nucleic acid testing with big data and full trip monitoring. The tracking capability is very powerful, and of course also reflects China's high-tech development in recent years. But these technologies did not originate in China, and the West has them too, but their use is constrained by privacy protections. Yao Yang, director of the National School of Development at Peking University, pointed out last year that, "China's relatively weak protection of personal privacy provides an advantage to China's AI technology development in some respects. It is nonetheless important for technology companies to be vigilant and prevent the emergence of a Leviathan-style state."[20] This "low-privacy advantage" is part of the "low-human-rights advantage" that I've referred to many times in recent years, and it's also being put to good use in the fight against the epidemic.

As a result of the widespread use of smartphones for big data tracking, some of China's poor and elderly, those who don't use mobile phones, those who only use old-fashioned mobile phones and won't use smartphones to access the Internet, and even (in some places) those who can access the Internet but won't accept Alipay, are now constantly running into difficulties, and even have a hard time surviving.

But what is sobering and frustrating is that, when a serious epidemic occurs, the soft-heartedness of democracies towards their citizens is not helpful in fighting the epidemic, while China's "ruthlessness," the harsh quarantines and tracking, has proven to be effective.

In fact, this is not difficult to understand. Logically speaking, there are only three ways for humans to deal with virulent infectious diseases: if you are already infected or are inevitably going to be infected, you have to use antibiotics or other means to destroy the germs or viruses in your body, which is curing the disease; if you cannot eliminate the disease, you have to rely on a vaccine, so as to avoid infection even if you come in contact with the pathogens, which is preventing the disease; and if you do not have a vaccine, then cutting off the spread of the pathogens is the only way forward.[21]

Antibiotics have been invented for most pathogenic bacteria, and vaccines have been invented for most germs and some viruses. But antibiotics are usually ineffective against viruses, and a vaccine against the coronavirus has not yet been invented (at the moment I am writing, in June 2020), so isolation is all we have.

But isolation entails the temporary restriction and elimination of some human rights, which, to put it bluntly, is tantamount to being imprisoned for no crime, in the public interest. So in simple terms of the ability to enforce isolation, low human rights countries do have an advantage, while high human rights countries have a disadvantage. This is what the logic dictates, and there's no way around it. Today's developed democracies are racking their brains to fight the epidemic, trying both "Zen" measures as well as iron-fisted control. Caught between the "left" (survival) and the "right" (human rights), between "dying from the pandemic" (rejecting isolation means the spread of the disease) and "dying of hunger" (long-term isolation means economic collapse), pure ideological differences no longer matter. Social Democratic Sweden and Trump, the socialism-hating American president, both went "Zen," while the high welfare countries of southern Europe and libertarian Switzerland chose "iron-handed" lockdowns. Yet as long as their practices remain democratic, they cannot be as "iron-fisted" as China, and while we cannot say that the two ways of fighting the pandemic completely failed, it is nonetheless true that, as of today, they pale in comparison to China's achievements.

In fact, shortly after Wuhan was locked down, I made a very "politically incorrect" but absolutely logical deduction: if a system could turn an infected area into an Auschwitz and send all the sick into the oven, then any infectious disease could be eliminated within its incubation period! Of course, in reality, no one would be so heartless.[22] But is it not true that the closer you are to such a system, the more "superiority in fighting epidemics" you have? Is there an optimal solution to this problem under the conditions that preserve the democratic system? That, I am afraid, is a thought that cannot be avoided in the wake of the terrible price paid by people around the world during this epidemic.

The Lesser of Two Evils:
A "Medieval Approach" to Combating the Epidemic?

In the past, I have used the concept of "low human rights advantage" to explain the phenomenon of certain low human rights countries taking advantage of the markets, investments, and innovations of high human rights countries, together with their own low costs, to achieve faster economic growth in the context of economic integration. Since I do not believe that economic growth justifies low human rights, I put "low human rights advantage" in quotation marks. However, in the fight against epidemics, where human lives are at stake, the low respect for human rights required for mandatory isolation may be an advantage that does not require such a qualification.

When Wuhan was first locked down, the West, still largely untouched by the virus, was shocked by the strength of China's forced quarantine. They said that China was adopting "medieval methods" to fight the epidemic. But China's later success largely quieted such accusations.

However, the "medieval" argument is not unfounded. From the perspective of values, it may be true that compulsory isolation temporarily diminishes certain human rights in ways that are necessary, but from a factual perspective, it is also true that compulsory isolation, especially the dual isolation system now widely used in China, traces its origins to Western medieval practices, helped along in this instance by modern technology. And it should be said that, in the absence of vaccines and effective antibiotics, "medieval means" are more important than modern science and technology in stopping the spread of the epidemic.

This is why Western developed countries have been more passive than China in the face of this spread, despite their higher level of modern science and technology.

As a result, Chinese public opinion is quite pleased with itself, and a popular saying has it that it is now time for the West to learn a "lesson" from China. Given that existing democratic institutions are not as effective as institutions with a low human rights advantage in combating the existing pandemic, is this true? Should the West "copy" China?

Of course not.

As a matter of fact, it's not as if "high human rights" have been around forever, in the West or China. Not only were there periods in Western history when human rights were undervalued, but anti-epidemic measures based on low human rights had already been developed as well, many "lessons" of which, strictly speaking, have been handed down to the present day. It's just that Westerners are now very reluctant to copy these medieval lessons. China, however, has been very successful. And as it turns out, until we have a better method, these medieval lessons represent the lesser of two evils and might be worth revisiting. It is true that modern-day humans are sometimes too conceited, not only in their arrogance towards "nature," as many have pointed out, but also towards the "old society." China has done a good job of reviewing these lessons, and the West should reflect on this. But China really has nothing to brag about.

China's success in fighting the epidemic has been technically based on two main factors: first, the mandatory wearing of masks, and second, mandatory physical isolation, especially the

The fact that Wu Liande did not believe in "rat-flea transmission" and correctly understood that it was "droplet transmission," and insisted on wearing masks, was certainly a brilliant idea and indeed worthy of the pride of Chinese people around the world. However, the use of masks as medical protection had already emerged internationally, and the mandatory use of masks as an emergency public health measure had already been practiced in various countries. During the Spanish Flu at the end of World War I, many countries, including the United States, required the wearing of masks.[26] Wu Liande understood that the plague in China's northeast was a respiratory infection and introduced and improved the mask (the built-in germicidal lining is considered to be the forerunner of the modern N95 mask), which was an outstanding contribution, but he was not the inventor of the medical mask, and that's all there is to it.

All peoples seem to have discovered social isolation, or even forced isolation, early on in their history. While ancient people may have had limited knowledge, understanding neither how diseases develop nor their basic causes, they could still easily observe that one person's illness was transmitted to the whole family and that contact with a sick person led to illness. This, coupled with the fact that "low human rights" was a common phenomenon in ancient times, made it easy to enforce compulsory isolation, which is why it was practiced almost by all peoples from very early on. This was especially true of virulent diseases like the plague and diseases like leprosy, the symptoms of which are immediately noticeable. In the *Old Testament*, "Leviticus" chapters 13 and 14 contain Moses' provisions for mandatory isolation of those with infectious skin diseases (generally considered to be leprosy) for seven to fourteen days, depending on the case, with continued isolation (perhaps for life) if no cure was apparent after fourteen days. Similar provisions are found in Chapter 5 of the "Book of Numbers." In fact, the chance of a fourteen-day recovery from leprosy under ancient conditions was slight, but Moses still allowed for the possibility of short-term quarantine, which must have been a merciful rule (whether it was effective is a different question). Later quarantines were often much more severe.

China's Qin dynasty built "pestilence areas," or leprosy quarantine spaces, within large-scale projects to punish prisoners (i.e., the equivalent of prisons or labor camps). In the "Answers to Questions on Legal Principles and Statutes" section of the Shuihudi Qin bamboo texts, we find the following passage:

> A has committed a crime punishable by remaining intact and being made a *ch'eng-tan* 城旦 [27]. Before his case has been decided, A proves to be a leper. Question: How is A to be sentenced? He is warranted to be banished to the lepers' place and made to live there. Some say: he is warranted to be banished to the lepers' place to be killed by drowning. [28]

In other words, prisoners suffering from leprosy were either put into isolation or executed while in isolation, which is a terrible type of "isolation." In the *Hanshu*'s "Chronicle of Emperor Ping," we find: "people with an epidemic disease should be left in an empty residence and supplied with medicine," which most people take to refer to epidemic prevention via quarantine, but a more humane type of isolation than what was practiced by the brutal Qin. In addition, the Persian medical sage Avicenna (980–1037) also mentioned the isolation of those suffering from infectious diseases in his *Canon of Medicine.*

In the past, there was a tradition of quarantining "dirty diseases" in the ethnic minority areas of China, and in the early 1960s, there was a popular ethnic minority movie called *Moya Dai,* which told the story of a "feudal tribal leader" who used quarantine to persecute people. In the Dai regions, there is a tradition of isolating "pipa ghosts," "pipa" being very close to the Thai word for "dirty disease," which is generally taken to mean leprosy. The film used the theory of class struggle in vogue at the time, and depicted the tribal leader as a landlord who labeled the Dai people who would not submit to his oppression "pipa ghosts" and arrested them on that basis. They were only liberated with the arrival of the Chinese Communist Party. Isolation is made out to be a terrible thing in the movie.

In fact, because isolation is coercive, it is sometimes used as a means of political persecution by despotic rulers under authoritarian conditions, resulting in the abuse or overuse of isolation. In the medieval West, there were cases of forced isolation in which "the suspension of personal liberty provided an opportunity for the use of special laws to suppress political opposition," in the words of one scholar.[29] During the Cold War, Soviet dissidents were "isolated" in psychiatric hospitals, and in the current epidemic, "isolation" was used as a means of "preventing" political opposition. The citizen journalists Chen Qiushi[30] and Fang Bin are also suspected of having suffered this fate in Wuhan because of having "spoken their conscience."

Nonetheless, in an age when antibiotics and vaccines are unavailable, forced isolation, as the lesser of two evils in terms of anti-epidemic measures, cannot be dispensed with. Although the film *Mayan Dai* makes the quarantine of "pipa ghosts" sound reprehensible, in fact, China's "new society" has been unable to do without such measures. As late as the Cultural Revolution period, we read in the memoirs of educated youth sent down to Xishuangbanna in Yunnan province that when they were assigned to a rural production team, the practice remained that when they contracted leprosy they were sent off to the leper's village, never to see their families again. But there were also people who suffered the same fate without having contracted leprosy. When I was in a Zhuang village in the Yunnan-Guizhou border region during the Cultural Revolution, I heard that there were still "leprosy villages" in the area.

The System of Dual Mandatory Isolation: Who is Copying Whom?

However, all of the references above refer to the confinement of the sick person, which in English is called "isolation" (I prefer the term "medical isolation"). Isolation of patients diagnosed with highly infectious diseases is usually uncontroversial or minimally controversial.[31] However, there is another important kind of isolation practiced in modern large-scale infectious disease prevention, namely the complete blockage of normal traffic, at the expense of work and productive activities, and the indiscriminate implementation of a compulsory quarantine—under observation—for outsiders who cannot be ensured to be uninfected or those who leave the infected area, until the expiration of the prescribed quarantine period, which is only lifted when it has been determined that there is no more infection. As a turning point in the fight against the epidemic, China's compulsory "urban lockdowns," as well as policies such as "quarantining all outsiders for fourteen days," are still being implemented in many areas even after the absolute "urban lockdowns" have been lifted. In English, this is called quarantine rather than isolation. The "China lesson" that many of our people are so happy to recommend to foreign countries is, in fact, mainly a reference to the highly coercive use of this technique. Some Chinese like to mock other countries for not being tough enough, or for deregulating too soon, as if a strictly enforced quarantine were a Chinese invention.

In fact, the opposite is true. Isolation is just as ancient in China as anywhere else, but not only are there no records of quarantine in ancient China, it also looks to have been rare in other non-Western traditions. As far as I can tell, quarantine is really a "lesson" from the medieval West.

Today, most international medical historians believe that quarantine dates back to the time of the Black Death, specifically to the case of Ragusa, a commercial city-state founded by Venetian Italians on the Adriatic coast (today's tourist attraction, the Croatian port city of Dubrovnik).[32] In ancient times, there was little population movement in agricultural areas, and it was not unheard of for people to simply close their doors and villages in times of crisis. But for a commercial city-state, prolonged isolation was tantamount to suicide, thus epidemics had to be prevented. On July 27, 1377, in response to the threat of a contagious epidemic disease (the Black Death), Ragusa issued the "Green Book," declaring that *"veniens de locis pestiferis non intret Ragusium nel districtum"* (those who come from plague-infested areas shall not enter Ragusa or its district), which was seen as the only way to prevent the plague. The three uninhabited outer islands of Mrkan, Bobari and Supetar were set aside for a thirty-day quarantine period, or *trentina* (Italian for thirty days), where foreign vessels—including people and merchandise—were required to dock. People from Ragusa were also forbidden all contact with the islands other than appointing people to deliver food and provide basic services. Later, Ragusa decided that overland travelers posed a greater risk of infection as they passed through their towns and villages, and imposed a forty-day (*quarantina* in Italian) isolation on overland visitors, which is where today's term "quarantine" comes from. Although the quarantine period was not necessarily forty days, everyone "copied Ragusa's lesson" and this is why we use the term today.[33]

In addition to quarantine, the chief physician of Ragusa at the time recommended the construction of isolation hospitals outside the city walls to treat sick citizens (or those suspected of being sick), which became known as isolation or medical quarantine. Thus was born the first dual quarantine system in history, consisting of quarantine and isolation.

These two segregated areas are collectively known as *lazaretto*, which is derived from the biblical story of St. Lazarus: poor Lazarus, covered with sores (alluding to leprosy), falls to the ground before a rich man's door, and both he and the rich man die. But while Lazarus was treated well by Abraham in the underworld, the rich man suffered the torments of purgatory. The rich man appealed to Abraham for help, and Abraham said that this was their reward for the respective happiness and pain the two had known in life, and added, "And besides all this, a great chasm has been fixed between us and you, so that even those who wish cannot cross from here to you, nor can anyone cross from there to us."[34] Lazarus was later revered as the patron saint of lepers, and the so-called "abyss of isolation" became a metaphor for anti-epidemic isolation. The Italian pronunciation of Lazarus, *Lazaretto*, then became the name for the quarantine areas and, along with quarantine, entered other European languages, including, somewhat later, English.

In 1403, inspired by the quarantine system of its colonial state, Ragusa, the Venetian government converted an island monastery in the southern part of its large lagoon into a quarantine hospital and named the island (Old) Lazaretto. In 1468 (some say 1423), another island in the northern part of the lagoon was converted into a quarantine site, and was named New Lazaretto. The old and new Lazaretto, one north of Venice and one south, were separated by the sea from the city of Venice. New Lazaretto was larger (nine hectares), and both outsiders and boats were quarantined there; Old Lazaretto was smaller (2.5 hectares), and housed both local patients and quarantined patients transferred from New Lazaretto if they fell ill. The former was similar to today's "centralized quarantine point" and the latter to a "modular hospital." The mortality rate in plague hospitals under those conditions was high, and the archaeological findings on Old Lazaretto show a large number of graves,[35] but not on New Lazaretto. This shows that the functions of the two were strictly differentiated.

This "Venetian system" became the model for other European countries. Over the next century, this system was adopted in Genoa, Pisa, and Ancona in Italy, as well as Marseilles in France, and was gradually copied by other European countries. In North America, the practices of quarantine and epidemic prevention were already in place during the colonial era, and large lazarettos appeared around the time of the founding of the United States: one was built on Bedloe Island (where today's Statue of Liberty is located) in 1738 in New York to combat smallpox and yellow fever epidemics. This place, which today symbolizes freedom, was a temporary detention center for those entering New York. In 1793, also because of the yellow fever epidemic, Philadelphia, then the capital of the newly established United States, built a lazaretto on the banks of the Delaware River, ten miles to the south, a structure that still stands today.[36]

Such quarantine measures were first introduced into the Persian Gulf by Iranians in 1772–1773, during the Iranian plague pandemic. Thereafter, these "lessons" have been copied to varying degrees outside of Europe, including by China. But today, even though China the student has surpassed its teachers in applying what gradually became the European system of dual quarantine and isolation, there is still no equivalent in the Chinese language for the two terms, and both are translated as "isolation" (*geli* 隔離), so if you don't pay attention to the context (as happens with machine translation), the English translation of the terms in Chinese disease control literature will often be incorrect, because it is impossible to distinguish between the two. However, the two are actually quite different: quarantine is for anyone suspected of possible infection, usually travelers, and is for a fixed period of time (although not forty days; we have set fourteen as the maximum for the coronavirus), and they must be isolated from both confirmed cases as well as those who are free of the disease or assumed to be free of the disease, otherwise there is a risk of cross-infection. Medical isolation, on the other hand, is only for confirmed cases and the length of time is indefinite (depending on recovery and contagion factors). Why is there no distinction between the two in Chinese? This is because the dual isolation system is a lesson we only recently learned, and we haven't yet perfected the terminology.

CHAPTER TWO

"Human Rights Derogations" during States of Emergency, and the Definition of Human Rights

Medical Progress and the Advancement of Human Rights: The Decline and Return of Forced Isolation

This dual system of quarantine played an increasing role in the fight against epidemics in the West during the 17th and 18th centuries, and into the 19th century. Isolated infectious disease hospitals and quarantine sites, many of which are now tourist attractions, were common across Europe at the time. There were several important reasons why forced quarantines were popular:

First, this period in the West marked the rise of "sovereign statehood" and "nation-state construction," in which the public functions of the state developed greatly. Many of the things that in the past had not been done by kings, but instead by lords, churches, and city-states, were now taken over by the state, which had the power, will, and resources to implement them.

Second, modern medicine had not yet developed fully at this time, and bacterial infectious diseases (plague, cholera, typhoid, leprosy, etc.) continued to pose the main threat to human life and health; there were no vaccines for most bacterial infectious diseases, to say nothing of antibiotics, which had not yet been invented. Viral infectious diseases were a lesser threat, but with the exception of the early history of smallpox vaccination, there was no vaccine for other viruses, and no drugs that were "anti-viral" in the same way that antibiotics would be "anti-bacterial." For this reason, compulsory isolation remained the main means of infectious disease prevention and control, and the role of the dual quarantine system could not be replaced.

Third, the progress of human rights in Europe during this period was still at the stage of fighting the nobility on the home front and Papal authority on the international front; the "alliance of citizens and kings" was still the main form of nation-state construction and most Western countries were still authoritarian states (or "absolutist" states). The resulting low state of human rights was also conducive to the implementation of forced isolation.

But by the end of the 19th century, and especially as Europe entered the 20th century, the situation changed drastically. First came tremendous progress in medicine, including the discovery of vaccines to prevent major bacterial infections and antibiotics to treat them, while smallpox, originally the worst of the viral infections, was gradually brought under control by vaccines, and the importance of compulsory isolation declined.

Second, although forced isolation had been indispensable in the past, modern medicine's understanding of pathogens made it seem ineffective. For example, the bubonic plague was mainly transmitted by rats and fleas, and even if isolation limited the contact between people, as long as rats and fleas were everywhere because of filthy living conditions, the disease could still spread largely unchecked. Therefore, despite the dual isolation system and the primitive "bird beak" masks of the Middle Ages, the spread of glandular plague could not be effectively eliminated. Thus in the late 19th century, things moved to the other extreme, and public health authorities stressed only rodent and flea eradication, and not isolation and wearing masks. This is why Mesnil and the other doctors opposed Wu Liande's use of masks. They did not know they were up against the pneumonic plague, which can be transmitted by droplets, and it was their loss. The ability to discriminate between the different types of plague and their appropriate responses came much later.

Third, the "low human rights advantage" of the time did not have enough high-tech support to facilitate close surveillance. Moreover, the hardships of forced isolation were likely to frighten the sick into desperate flight, which would spread the disease even further. This is one of the reasons why quarantines were abandoned.

Last and certainly most important, with the progress of liberal democracy since the 19th century, authoritarian nation-states and "absolutist" states increasingly became a thing of the past, and human rights claims increased. The rise in dissatisfaction with the violation to human rights caused by forced isolation, and, in particular, the growing criticism of the misuse of isolation by authoritarian regimes for political persecution,[1] also put an end to the "low human rights advantage" that facilitated the imposition of forced isolation and has led to a growing reluctance on the part of democracies to impose such measures, and the taboos against massive and intense physical isolation have continued to grow.

The classic quarantine islands of Lazaretto in southern Europe, which had been popular for centuries under the "Venetian system," were abandoned one after the other. Venice's New Lazaretto was converted into a military fortress during the Napoleonic era, and the one in Dubrovnik (then Ragusa), considered the birthplace of the quarantine, was also turned into another kind of public health facility during the same period. Many lazarettos were abandoned or converted to other uses during that period, not unrelated to the changes brought about by the French Revolution. In the words of the Italian historian Eugenia Tognotti:

> The intensified use of quarantine and isolation went contrary to the establishment of civil rights and the growth of personal liberty fostered by the French Revolution of 1789. In Britain, liberal reformers challenged quarantine and mandatory smallpox vaccination.... This phenomenon affected many European countries.[2]

Dissatisfaction with forced isolation was particularly evident in the case of leprosy. Unlike acute infectious diseases such as plague, where death rates are high and survivors recover quickly, "quarantine" for leprosy—a chronic disease—was tantamount to a life sentence. In addition, the traditional understanding of leprosy was easily "expanded."[3] In contrast to many ancient traditions of outright discrimination against people affected by leprosy, medieval Christian attitudes toward leprosy were ambivalent and somewhat reminiscent of what we saw with the lockdown of Wuhan during the coronavirus outbreak. On the one hand, the image of Wuhan was praised to the skies, and the media blathered on endlessly with talk of a "City of Heroes" and cries of "Go Wuhan!" On the other hand, each individual Wuhan person was regarded as a "source of contagion" and discriminated against, and "Wuhaners" outside of Wuhan were like rats scurrying across the street, reported on and arrested everywhere. It was the same in medieval Europe, where St. Lazarus, the patron saint of lepers, was considered more holy than the rich and favored by the gods, but where actual lepers were worse off than prisoners. With the invention of effective treatments in the 1940s, the threat of leprosy infection has been almost eliminated, and there are movements championing the rights of those who suffer from leprosy, with quarantine sites in developed countries being largely eliminated and even campaigns launched seeking apologies and compensation for victims of previous quarantines.

A typical case is Japan, where leprosy quarantine laws were not formally abolished until the 1990s, and the West, which had eliminated such quarantine practices in the 1960s, considered the Japanese case an "unprecedented violation of human rights," even though Japan made progressively less use of the quarantine laws. In 2001, nearly 2,000 former leprosy patients sued the Government of Japan. An independent court ruled that the Government must

the wake of the epidemics of SARS and influenza A, the Italian epidemiological historian Eugenia Tognotti noted in 2013:

> A new chapter in the history of quarantine opened in the early twenty-first century as traditional intervention measures were resurrected in response to the global crisis precipitated by the emergence of SARS, an especially challenging threat to public health worldwide. SARS, which originated in Guangdong Province, China, in 2003, spread along air-travel routes and quickly became a global threat because of its rapid transmission and high mortality rate and because of the lack of protective immunity in the general population....In China, police cordoned off buildings, organized checkpoints on roads, and even installed Web cameras in private homes. There was stronger control of persons in the lower social strata (village-level governments were empowered to isolate workers from SARS-affected areas). Public health officials in some areas resorted to repressive police measures, using laws with extremely severe punishments, against those who violated quarantine.[8]

The reference to "in the past" and "the resurrection of traditional interventions" actually refers to the return of the "low human rights advantage" of the medieval fight against epidemics. "In the face of a dramatic health crisis, individual rights have often been trampled in the name of public good....This feature, almost inherent in quarantine, traces a line of continuity from the time of plague to the 2009 H1N1 pandemic."[9] From today's perspective, however, both SARS and H1N1 are trivial. It was only in March of 2020, during the Italian "lockdowns" in Italy, that Tognotti really saw the return of the medieval "Venetian system" she had studied in the past:

> As an epidemiological historian, I have tried to imagine the reactions of men and women who had experienced devastating epidemics. But I never imagined that I would find myself living in history as the lockdowns spread throughout Italy....But COVID-19 has once again emphasized the fact that epidemics are not a memory from the pre-industrial past. The severe measures adopted in China strongly suggest that the ancient, basic concept of quarantine is still valid. In the absence of a targeted vaccine, general preventive interventions still have to be relied upon. The strategies recently adopted in Italy have their roots in the past. From the onset of the Black Death in 1347–48, Italian cities implemented a complex health defense system, which was an example to other European countries. The cornerstones of this health defense system lay in quarantine, sanitary cordons, lazarettos (quarantine stations), disinfection and social regulation of the population at risk.[10]

"In fact, the first to refine a system of defense against disease was Venice." Today, Italy, which enjoys robust human rights, cannot impose isolation measures with the same intensity as in the past: at the time, Venice required foreign sailors to be locked in a closed room and speak to someone positioned outside the window who recorded what they said. This was "safe distance" as understood then. "The recommended distance for coronavirus in the guidelines today is one meter. I could not verify in the historic records what distance was suggested by the Venetian health magistrates!"[11]

The Siracusa Principles and Human Rights "Derogations"

In fact, scholars of disease control and officials in various countries generally agreed throughout the 20th century that human "medical progress" was still limited, and that the past system of isolation could not be easily abandoned. This is especially true at the international level. It is well known that progress in human rights has been significantly slower internationally than within democracies; freedom of movement, for example, is not a problem within democracies, but it is still difficult internationally. Thus in the 20th century, quarantine and isolation developed mainly at the international level. A multilateral convention on international health was concluded in Paris in 1912, and another such convention was signed in Paris in 1926 to replace that of 1912. These conventions both had provisions for international cooperation in the application of quarantine and isolation. At the same, human rights considerations are also an international trend. Following the adoption of the United Nations International Covenant on Civil and Political Rights (ICCPR), in 1984 the International Institute for Criminal Justice and Human Rights in Siracusa, Italy, and the Economic and Social Council of the United Nations, adopted the Siracusa Principles, which introduced certain limitations and "derogations" from the human rights standards of the ICCPR, which left room for the mandatory system of dual isolation.[12]

The Siracusa Principles state that public health may be used as a basis for restricting certain human rights if the state needs to take measures "aimed at preventing disease or injury or providing care for the sick and injured." However, human rights restrictions (such as isolation) must be "strictly necessary," which means that they must: respond to urgent public or social needs (in matters of health); be proportional in their pursuit of legitimate objectives (preventing the spread of infectious diseases); represent the least restrictive means necessary to achieve the purpose of the restriction; follow the law in their framing and implementation; be neither arbitrary nor discriminatory; restrict only rights within the jurisdiction of the state seeking to impose the restriction.

In addition, certain scholars have identified the following ethical requirements for the implementation of isolation measures, based on the Siracusa Principles and other United Nations regulations: all restrictive measures must be fully supported by data and scientific evidence; all information must be made available to the public; all actions must be clearly explained to those whose rights are restricted and to the public; all actions are subject to periodic review and reconsideration.

Finally, the state has a moral obligation to provide certain guarantees: infected people will not be threatened or mistreated; basic needs such as food, water, medical care, and preventive care will be provided; communication with relatives and caregivers will be allowed; restrictions on liberty will apply regardless of social considerations; the sick will be fairly compensated for financial and material losses, including wages.[13]

As a number of scholars have concluded, quarantine and other public health tools remain at the core of public health preparedness in the face of new challenges posed by the emergence of infectious diseases in the 21st century, and the increasing risk of their rapid spread. In this regard, attention must be paid to the valuable lessons of the past. At the same time, given their very nature, vigilance is required in order to avoid prejudice and intolerance. Public trust must be sustained through regular, transparent, and comprehensive communication to balance the risks and benefits of public health interventions, and successfully respond to public health emergencies.[14]

It is clear that these provisions are intended to reconcile the principles of human rights in the modern civilized world with the existence of the age-old system of compulsory quarantine, which one cannot, in fact, abolish when antibiotics and vaccines cannot be counted on. But as decades of practice have shown, achieving this balance is often a matter of wishful thinking, and in 2013, scholars pointed out that in Kenya and Canada's efforts to combat the spread of drug-resistant tuberculosis, there were cases where the free movement of the source of infection was considered a threat to public health and safety, resulting in the involuntary detention of people, in a breach of the Siracusa principles. The article, entitled "Failing Siracusa: Governments' Obligations to Find the Least Restrictive Options for Tuberculosis Control,"[15] demonstrates that the Siracusa Principles do not fully resolve the "lesser of two evils" problem.

And the current coronavirus pandemic has only heightened the problem.

The undeniable fact is that, despite its many mistakes, China succeeded in controlling the epidemic by using extreme coercive measures that go far beyond the Siracusa Principles. Democracies such as European countries, America, Japan and Australia, however, have been significantly less coercive than China in terms of these principles, and have had difficulty controlling the epidemic. As time goes by, insufficiently coercive measures may also have the effect of doing more harm than good to the economy, even as they fail to eradicate the epidemic. Once the dilemma of "human rights" versus "no humans left" becomes that of "death by starvation" versus "death from the virus," the choice is all the more difficult. In retrospect, it is certain that survival ("humans left") is more important than human rights. The fierce criticism of the early days of China's "Wuhan lockdown" has almost disappeared now that the effects have become clear. Knowing what we know now, if we could turn back the clock, I think European and American governments would have chosen to copy China's "lesson" at the beginning of the epidemic (of course, this in fact would have meant reviewing the "lesson" from their own medieval experience). Whether the democratic system would allow them to do so is another question. But today, as the second wave of the coronavirus hits already devastated economies, the dilemma of choosing between "dying from the virus" (where continued laxity worsens the still spreading disease) and "death by starvation" (where renewed control leads to the collapse of an already weakened economy) is all the more painful.

This raises an acute question: in what kind of emergency can human rights be "limited" or "derogated from" (in the language of the Siracusa Principles) and to what extent, and can these limitations or derogations be imposed "efficiently" enough to be effective? Must democracies be so incompetent in the face of an emergency? "Live free or die" is certainly timeless and of universal value as a slogan for freedom, and as a choice for some individuals can be admirable. But for human society, survival is more important than freedom (especially high levels of freedom, such as the freedom of getting together to have fun during an epidemic), and jeopardizing public safety for one's own freedom is contrary to universal values (not just "Asian values"). Of course, the current coronavirus epidemic may not be the most serious challenge; after all, the death rate is not very high. But what if the death rate had been like that of the Black Death, and there were still no antibiotics or vaccines available?

It is also possible to imagine an even more extreme scenario: what if the "conspiracy theories," which are now commonplace in both China and the West, were to prove true in the future: democracies and totalitarian states would unfortunately really be engaged in a "virus war" against each other, with each viciously attacking the other with "contagions." Don't tell me that it's technically or humanly impossible; making logical deductions on the basis of the current pandemic, what are the odds of democracy's survival? Are they greater than for totalitarianism? Obviously, if we support democracy, not necessarily seeking to develop it further, but supporting it simply in terms of the sustainability of its achievements so far, we cannot avoid this serious question: can the survival of the democratic system depend solely on the goodwill of others, and even the enemy?

Rights, Legitimacy, and the Good: On the Definition of Human Rights and the Legitimacy of "Derogations"

Recently, the Chinese government has seized the momentum of victory in the fight against the pandemic. It held a series of international video seminars on "global epidemic prevention and control and human rights safeguards," strongly criticizing the West both for its ineffectiveness in fighting the epidemic and for blaming China, and accusing the West of "disregarding human rights," the same accusation the West often directs at China. On the Internet, others have applied the phrase "low human rights advantage," which I coined, as far as I can tell, to the West, saying that their "low human rights advantage" is reflected in the West's refusal to adopt the harsh Chinese approach to fighting the epidemic, despite the spread of the disease and the increasing death toll—which is, of course, a mockery.

Undoubtedly, the West's incompetence and ineffectiveness in the face of the epidemic should be criticized, just as China's success in fighting the epidemic through lockdowns should be recognized and emulated. But what this success has to do with the relationship between ineffectiveness and human rights is quite the opposite, in my view. As a matter of fact, the saying that was popular around the world during the campaign against the pandemic was "quarantine, no human rights; no quarantine, no humans left." Taken together with the Siracusa Principles, the above-mentioned UN statement that in the event of a forced quarantine, a temporary "limitation and derogation" should be imposed on a certain range of human rights, both express the high-level contradiction between "human rights" and "human survival" during states of emergency, and the need for a temporary freeze on certain human rights to assure that priority be given to human survival. It should be acknowledged that low human rights have indeed been a major advantage in China's successful fight against the pandemic. To put it another way, high human rights have become a disadvantage for the West in its fight. The high priority accorded to human rights, regardless of the state of emergency, has severely hamstrung public power in the West, meaning that coercive measures that should have been implemented were not implemented, or were implemented too late, or were removed too soon, or were not applied properly. In this global pandemic, Westerners have paid a very heavy price for their freedom and human rights. This is an important point to reflect on in the face of this pandemic.

In recent years, my argument concerning China's "low human rights advantage" has aroused heated controversy. Some think that the term "low human rights" belittles China, while others think that using the term "advantage" justifies China's low human rights. Others point out that there is too much controversy over the definitions and standards of human rights, and that we should not discuss their "superiority" or "inferiority" lightly. In fact, I am clearly aware of and do not ignore the human rights debate; if we indulged our pedantic impulses, we could easily produce several books. At the same time, I don't think it is difficult to explain what "human rights" are in common sense terms. It is just that if we invest rights with value, and decide that "human rights" are unconditionally regarded as a good thing, then conflicts between different values will lead to a confusion of meanings: if there is a right that we should *not* have, then is it not a right? And if it is not a "right," then what is it? Surely not an "obligation."

In fact, "human rights" are the rights that belong to people, and "people" clearly means the individual, not the "state" or the "nation," or anything else. The reason is simple: the "rights of the state" are usually described by the term "sovereignty," and the debate over which has priority, sovereignty or human rights, no matter which we choose, shows that the two are not the same thing. Not to mention the fact that countries generally seen as disregarding human rights, such as Nazi Germany, usually give great prominence to the "rights of the state" and emphasize the dependence of the individual on the state. The word now used for rights in modern Chinese—*quanli* 權利—meant something different in classical Chinese, but now is seen as the equivalent of "right" in English: if a certain person can choose to do, or not to do, a certain thing, then we say that that person has the right to do that thing, and if he or she cannot do that thing, then he or she does not have that right. If that person *has* to do the thing, then it is an obligation, and not a right.

The debate about human rights is, in the final analysis, not about whether the ability to do or not to do a certain thing is a "right," or whether or not it is a "human right," but rather if the rights themselves should be granted. For example, I believe that democracies should not grant an unconditional right for citizens to bear arms. But the reason should be that this is a right one should not have, and not that it is not a human right. To cite opposition to the right of citizens to bear arms as the reason to brag about the state's unlimited monopoly on, and the use of, violence, as some people do in China, and to call this a "high human right," is the height of absurdity.

Of course, such human rights are not always recognized even in the developed democratic world. The reason is that with more gun owners, there will be more gun-related deaths and injuries, in the same way that with more cars, there will be more deaths and injuries due to accidents. But if the number of car crashes is not a measure of human rights, what does the number of gun deaths have to do with a "human rights record"?

But it is also important to note that the high incidence of gun-related crime, while not a human rights issue, is one of the ills of American society. It is untenable to justify the right to bear arms today by saying "that's the way things have always been." Today's United States is not the same as it was in the colonial era. The days when settlers carried guns for self-defense in a lawless state and resisted the King's ban on guns to protect their dignity are long gone. Arguments about protection against wild animals, attacks by Native Americans, and defense against tyranny no longer hold water, and the idea that "standing armies are always tyrannical" has long been disproven in a democracy. Since the misuse of firearms has become a danger to law and order, there is more harm than good in having guns as an individual right. It is debatable how to ban guns in a society such as the United States, where guns have long been commonplace, and if things are mismanaged so that the good people handed in their guns while the bad guys keep theirs, the situation would be even worse. But strict gun control is clearly the way to go.

The point is, the right to bear arms is a human right, but it is no longer an "inherent right." Whether a certain phenomenon is a human right is a factual judgment, and whether it should be a human right is a value judgment. But the problem is: the word "right" in English also means "legitimate" or "lawful," which seems to be a positive word, so whether something is a human right becomes a value judgment instead of a factual judgment. At the same time, the English-speaking world has long had the expression "right isn't necessarily good," so it is logically possible to have "bad rights." However, the prevailing opinion on the relationship between right and good has always been that right takes precedence over good as a fundamental issue in ethics.[16] Although I accept this in general (because not accepting it would mean that arbitrary human rights violations on the grounds of what someone calls "goodness" would become the norm), in an English context where "right" in the sense of legitimate and "right" in the sense of a human right are the same word, if we changed "right takes precedence over good" to "*rights* take precedence over good," there is a danger that the rights of the individual would expand so infinitely that they would break through the boundaries of the "rights of the many." After all, there are limits to individual rights; even if the human rights recognized by the United States currently include the individual right to bear arms, does it follow that the United States would recognize the individual right to possess nuclear arms? Naturally, the reason for not recognizing such a right is not that the individual right to nuclear weapons is not "good" (just as "not good" acts committed by gun owners do not negate the individual right to bear arms in the view of the gun advocates), but only that it is not "legitimate." It goes too far, so even those who are pro-gun rights can't be pro-nuclear weapon rights.

Obviously, it is possible for rights to be not only "not good" but also "not right." Maybe it has to do with the nature of the English language, but while Americans are very active in discussing the idea that a "right isn't good," they have a hard time with the notion of rights that aren't "right." As a result, some people wind up unconditionally affirming and defending human rights that are not "right" in the sense of being improper (such as the "right not to wear a mask"), or, refuse to "derogate" from rights which in normal times are legitimate and proper, but which should be limited in times of emergency, thus doing harm to general social welfare. Others, on the contrary, in order to deny these same rights (i.e., people who refuse to recognize the "right not to wear a mask"), refuse to acknowledge them as human rights, to the point of opposing "excessive" human rights as if they were no rights at all, and regard the necessary "derogations" from human rights in certain states of emergency as human rights themselves. In this way, not only does "derogation" become the norm, but even legitimate human rights—from which there is no derogation under the norm—are absurdly labeled as "disregard for human rights." This creates a situation in which those who oppose human rights in normal times wind up adapting to the state of emergency because they can "derogate" at will, to the point of becoming defenders of human rights!

In fact, since "right" is the ability to "do or not to do" something, it is synonymous with "freedom." Take isolation during an epidemic as an example. Under normal circumstances I can either stay home or go out, which means that I have the right, or the freedom, to choose between the two. However, during an epidemic I am asked to be in "home isolation," at which point I lose my "right" to go outside (or, conversely, if I am put in "medical quarantine" in a public health facility, I lose my right to stay home), and in these cases staying home (or remaining in the medical facility) become "obligations" that I have to fulfill, and no longer my right. Obviously, in such a situation, my rights, or human rights, suffer an extreme "derogation." Because of the needs imposed by the pandemic, this temporary restriction of rights is proper, and if I were to insist on the normal exercise of my rights in this situation it would be improper. However, you cannot argue that my human rights are better "protected" in this situation, just as you cannot argue that I am "freer" in isolation.

In the video seminar on the "prevention and control of global epidemics and the protection of human rights," that I mentioned above, many people claimed that China's draconian measures reflected respect for the right to life. In fact, I do not disagree that these measures were correct and that their implementation is a sign of respect for "life." But if we are to say that the right to life is respected, then we must ask who is the subject of this right. If we consider it to be a living person, it obviously cannot be said that forcing that person into isolation is respecting his or her individual rights, although it could be argued that it would be respecting the public interest.

Because the right to life in the strict sense must be a right that living beings possess, it is not always the same thing as life itself. A typical example is that some advanced countries commonly recognized as having high human rights, such as Switzerland, the Netherlands, and Canada, have now passed laws to allow legal euthanasia, i.e., to allow terminally ill people who feel that they would rather die than live, to choose to give up their lives in an appropriate manner to end their suffering. Conservatives can criticize this as a lack of respect for life, but not for the "right to life." For if a person is "forced to live," then although they have life, it is not their right to live, but merely their duty. It is true that

The right to subsistence and the right to speak are what we call negative rights, freedoms that "cannot be denied (or taken away)." The traditional "right wing" in the West, or those who preach laissez-faire, often only recognize these types of human rights. But there is in fact another category of "positive rights" pursued by the Western "left" that are seen as "socialist," such as affirmative action programs seeking to redress the conditions of African-Americans, a focus of attention in the United States at present, or the social security and welfare rights enumerated in the United Nations International Covenant on Economic, Social and Cultural Rights, or, once again, the Siracusa Principles, which refer to "basic needs such as food, water, medical care and health care" that must be guaranteed even in times of epidemic, and the idea "the sick will receive fair compensation for financial and material losses, including wages," etc. These rights seek the freedom to demand certain things.[23] Since the realization of such demands requires the government to expend a considerable amount of power, accomplishes a certain redistribution of wealth, and inevitably contradicts the "negative rights" of at least part of the population (e.g., paying high taxes to finance high welfare), the right wing tends to reject such appeals.

But even from the left's standpoint, the proposition that "the welfare state requires greater power and positive rights require the redistribution of wealth" cannot be twisted around to argue that "great power is the welfare state and heavy taxation is the guarantee of positive rights." In fact, the subjects of what the left calls positive rights are still free individuals; and what they call big government still means an accountable government, a government that receives its power from the people and is answerable to the people. "Positive rights" mean that I have the right to ask for guarantees, that the government has a duty to provide services, that I do not have to "thank" the government for these services because it is their duty to deliver them, and that if it does not, it will be held accountable, which could mean losing power. If, on the other hand, "welfare" is an imperial gift for which subjects must give thanks without demanding accountability, then this is the "imperial state," the exact opposite of the welfare state, and what the imperial subjects receive has nothing to do with the "positive rights" of citizens, to say nothing of human rights.

And just as the "right to subsistence" is not the same as subsisting, the "right to welfare" is not the same as enjoying welfare. To take Yang Guifei as an example yet again, when she was in favor, she not only subsisted, but enjoyed extreme luxury, an extremely high level of welfare that extended to her family and relatives, and she was envied to the point that Chinese of that time wanted to have daughters rather than sons. But once she fell out of favor, living in a cold palace and washing her own clothes were the least of her problems, as her death and the extinction of her family were distinct possibilities. What is more important to stress is that, once what appears to be the same thing changes from a situation of "the people's rights and government's responsibilities" to one of "the government's rights and people's responsibilities," the meaning is completely reversed: the people's demand for the government to guarantee employment is a positive human right, what we call welfare, but the government's demand for people to work is called corvée labor or labor camps. When the poor demand to be taken out of the slums to live in safe housing, that is called welfare, but when the government demolishes the slums and evicts the "low-end population," that is called tyranny. When the homeless demand shelter from the government, this is called relief aid, while the government forcibly detains what it calls "unchecked migration." This is what Karl Marx called "bloody legislation!"[24] In the same way that euthanasia is a negative human right (note that negative is not pejorative here), the denial of a speedy death to the criminal sentenced to the death of one thousand cuts is inhumane; in the same way that freedom of speech is the human right to express oneself, being "deprived of silence" and forced to speak is a violation of human rights.

Therefore, any human right, be it a negative right prized by the "rightists" or a positive right dear to the "leftists," is in fact premised on free human rights. This is the reason why I can rise above "left and right" to talk about the existence or lack thereof of human rights, and the level at which human rights exist. Of course, their existence—or lack thereof—and the level at which they exist are all judgments based in fact, while whether we should have them, and at what level, are value judgments. Whether it is the negative human right of "not being deprived of something" (which is often seen as the human rights of the right) or the positive human right of "demanding something" (often seen as the human rights of the left), both have limits, and in normal times we cannot say that the "greater" a right is, the "better" it is, and in extraordinary times, "derogations" may be required from both types of rights. There is also a contradiction between these two human rights: in constitutional democracies, when the poor demand their positive human rights to "high welfare," this will inevitably conflict with the wealthy's demand for their negative human rights "not be deprived (by high taxes) of their right to keep their money" (under non-democratic conditions, however, when rulers practice extortion in the name of self-interest, the conflict between the poor's demand for welfare and the wealthy's demand for limited taxes does not always occur). In a normal constitutional state, it is precisely this contradiction that leads to the left replacing the right, and vice versa. In a state of emergency, however, where both human rights may require temporary derogations, political temperatures rise quickly, and the different issues that this gives rise to in different political systems are well worth examining.

CHAPTER THREE

States of Emergency and Political Institutions

When "High Human Rights" Threaten the "Survival" of Human Beings: An Analysis of the "Titanic Story"

Human rights are rights, the ability to "do or not to do something," or in other words, freedom. And in all countries throughout history, prison (deprivation of liberty) has been used as a punishment for criminals, so it is clear that freedom is a human desire and human rights are universal values. Even a fascist dictator will defend his own freedom—it's just that he will deprive others of their freedom and violate their human rights, extending to a broad deprivation of the right to life of others, to the outrage of all.

But just because everyone wants to be free does not mean that is *all* they want, and that nothing else matters. In fact, while "live free or die" is certainly a celebration and encouragement of the spirit of freedom, when faced with the choice between death with freedom and life without it, most of us, following human nature, choose the latter. Moreover, absolute freedom does not exist, although authoritarian arguments that deny different degrees of freedom or even defend an absolute lack of freedom because there is no "absolute freedom" are absurd, but everywhere and throughout history, human beings, in pursuit of survival and other public values, have surrendered part of their freedom. At the same time, freedom also has two kinds of "externalities," positive and negative: instances in which people fail to compromise their freedom to achieve a common goal[1] and those in which people ignore the freedom of others after having obtained their own freedom, should both be prevented. The Chinese scholar Yan Fu (1854–1921) translated the title of John Stuart Mill's *On Liberty* as "On the Boundaries Between the Rights of the Group and the Individual," which I think is very accurate. The essence of constitutional democracy is to strictly observe the boundaries of the rights of the group and the individual. The community wants democracy, and the individual wants freedom. The two domains have their own rules, which should not be confused and especially not reversed. Public affairs cannot be "freely" managed by individuals without a public mandate, even if they are sages, and personal affairs cannot be left to the "public power," even if it is a democratic regime. This establishes "rights boundaries" for both freedom and democracy.

As far as the relationship between freedom and survival is concerned, "the right to subsistence" is not the same "subsistence," as discussed above. Opportunities to live a life of luxury through relying on others, like Yang Guifei, the "golden bird in a cage" without human rights, are both rare and unreliable (as the tragedy that befell her at Maweipo proves), so human rights and survival, high human rights and a superior quality of life are usually highly correlated.

But it is different during a state of emergency. When we say "quarantine, no human rights; no quarantine, no humans left," what we mean is that on such occasions, the normal "rights boundaries between the community and the self" must be adjusted. "Derogations" to human rights made in the public interest, diminishing the realm of the individual and limiting individual freedom are all necessary to ensure our common survival.

In fact, the "rights boundaries between the group and the individual" often need to be fine-turned even under normal conditions. I have argued that the interaction between "left and right" in a democratic system serves this function. Generally when the left comes to power, in economic terms it tends to expand the realm of the group and shrink that of the individual, and in ethical terms, will expand the realm of the individual and shrink that of the group. The right, by contrast, in economic terms will expand the individual realm and in ethical terms expand that of the group. The mechanism of democracy is still necessary to decide who will be in power. Of course, democracy can only determine the rights boundaries between the group and the individual in terms of the fuzzy areas of contention defined by the modern left and right, while the basic divisions between public and private, including questions of freedom of speech, cannot be defined by direct democracy or the constitution. The most basic human rights can in principle only be regarded as self-evident truths.

However, in states of emergency, where societies are faced with the difficult choice between the lesser of two evils, the normal logic just discussed often does not apply.

More than twenty years ago, I used the "Titanic story" to illustrate this point in another context. In a nutshell, the Titanic was sinking and there were only enough lifeboats for the women and children. Can you use your right to exist to force your way on? In other words, when the crisis is so severe that it threatens the survival of all, even the "fundamental value" of an individual's right to live is not "absolute." Some may say: what actually happened on the Titanic? Others say people did not behave as nobly as the legend suggests. It is true that there are a number of different accounts of the Titanic incident, and it is neither possible nor necessary to make a historical examination here, but we can confine our analysis to what is known as "Titanic literature." Because this treatment of the legend is generally accepted, it reflects a kind of judgment as to "how things should be." This judgment itself deserves careful analysis. One can doubt whether, as the Titanic was sinking, they truly managed to cling to the principle of "women and children first," but no one seems to think that women and children should *not* have been given priority, nor does anyone say that the priority of women and children is only a "Western value," and that Chinese would have abandoned women and children in a mad scramble for the lifeboats. So the "Titanic question" can be judged on its own, apart from the specific event, and discussions of the questions can transcend cultural differences.

The point raised by the Titanic story is to say, in effect, that the right to exist in the usual sense of the word may be restricted when the crisis is so severe that it is a matter of life and death. Even then, of course, the question of the "rules of fairness" remains. The Titanic is in trouble and the right to existence is restricted, but restricted to whom? If the principle is women and children first, then if you're not a woman or a child, too bad. I wrote at the time:

> An essential element of liberalism is the emphasis on the "rights boundaries between the group and the individual." The group talks about democracy, while the individual talks about freedom. However, the above example illustrates that the boundaries of the public and private domains are not so absolute. In the extreme case of the Titanic, even the most basic private right, the right to subsist, is handled by the group. But this does not mean that it was handled arbitrarily; the group also has to be governed by rules, and the basic rule is democracy. Although the "women and children first" principle seen in the tragedy of the Titanic was not the result of a vote, it was clearly accepted as such, and anyone violating the principle would have been stopped by the rest of the group.[2]

In fact, it now seems that this last argument of mine does not hold water. Since "women and children first" had not been decided by a vote, we cannot see it as the product of "group democracy." The fact that everyone accepted the captain's decision and cooperated with him does not prove that the decision was democratic, otherwise any tyrannical act that did not result in public revolt would be equally "democratic." In fact, the Titanic story does suggest that the rights of individuals in states of emergency are extremely curtailed by the public interest, but the public interest is not decided by democratic processes. In other words, during an emergency, not only does the individual sacrifice his or her freedom, the community also sacrifices its democracy. The only reason for this is if, during an emergency situation, we allow ourselves the "freedom" to fight for a small number of lifeboats, it may wind up being the case that no one gets on, and the same is true for the time it takes to carry out a "democratic" vote. So the captain has to decide. This has nothing to do with "culture," nor does it have anything to do with "political philosophy." The passengers may be libertarians who, when they are on land, argue in favor of gun rights. They may also be progressives, who argue that even the captain of the ship should be elected. But when the Titanic hit the iceberg, they all had to put their "doctrines" aside.

Yet, why is the captain's decision, which both denies freedom and tramples on democracy, accepted by all? What values would explain this acceptance, whether we mean by the passengers at the time, or others, East and West, who heard the story later? At the time, I came up with two possibilities, one of which no longer seems valid (the "democratic" explanation mentioned above), leaving only one: "The captain of the ship who made the decision was not himself a woman or a child, which means he sacrificed his own right to exist, and it is this sacrifice by some for the sake of others that makes the decision seem acceptable. If the captain himself and his friends and family had rushed onto the lifeboat, the story would have turned out differently."

This is, in fact, an important rule of "public disaster ethics." We will come back to it later.

A Historical Review of "Dictatorship" and "Autocracy"

In fact, the shortcomings of democratic systems in coping with states of emergency is nothing new. From the earliest use of the political notions of "democracy" and "republic" in ancient Greece and Rome, sustainable democracy has been associated with special arrangements for dealing with states of emergency. The Roman Republic's dictator system (military dictatorship) was a typical example. This was originally an emergency institution, created by the Roman Republic, in which the normal function of the republic was interrupted in the event of war, and military commanders were granted short-term arbitrary powers not constrained by Roman law. At the end of the war the dictator stepped down and handed power back to the Senate, which promised not to hold him accountable for his actions during the dictatorship. According to the customs of the time, the dictator's mandate was limited to six months, and its renewal required a new authorization from the Senate. But toward the end of the Republic the dictator ceased to respect the rules, and by the time of Octavian he was simply called head of state (*princeps*), and as Rome entered its imperial phase, the title of "dictator" ceased to exist.

The word "dictatorship" in Western languages is derived from the Roman dictator system. Obviously, because dictatorship was a state of emergency in wartime, it was different from autocracy, and conventional authoritarian regimes seen in Persia and elsewhere, including those in imperial Rome. In the later periods of the Roman Empire, and in the medieval and Byzantine periods, when "despotism" became the norm, the word dictator was extremely rare. It was not until the violent revolutions of modern times that the term was used again in its original sense, with Cromwell in the English Revolution and the Jacobin system in the French Revolution being two examples that are often mentioned. Robespierre, for example, stated that dictatorship is a state of war between liberty and its enemies, while constitutionalism is a free system of government in times of victory and peace.[3]

Thus the first thing we see is that what we call dictatorship is a kind of wartime interruption of democracy, or in other words, that if there is dictatorship, then there is no democracy, so the term "democratic dictatorship" makes no sense—it's as if we were to say "black-colored white." Secondly, dictatorship is also incompatible with the rule of law in peacetime, and Lenin was right when he said that "dictatorship...is rule unrestricted by any laws,"[4] which was the original meaning of the term. Of course a dictatorship cannot be a lawless jungle state, but it requires the replacement of the rule of law and the high human rights usually associated with the rule of law with certain military control measures. Thirdly, a dictatorship is a temporary measure associated with a state of emergency (usually war), a short-term suspension of the republican system, rather than a normal way of governing, unlike "autocracy."

The reason Marx and Engels spoke only of the "dictatorship" of the proletariat and never of the "autocracy" of the proletariat, the reason they spoke of the "dictatorship" only in the context of the 1848 revolution and the "civil war" of the Paris Commune, and the reason the leftist organizations of Western and Central Europe in the era and under the direction of Marx and Engels did not include the term "dictatorship" in their manifestos or even general documents was that such a temporary measure was seen as similar to those employed in the context of the Roman Republic, an interlude that had nothing to do with the republican idea. According to the Russian dissident scholar Roy Medvedev (b. 1925), when Marx and Engels spoke of the "dictatorship of the proletariat," "they used the word 'dictatorship' in the ancient Roman sense."[5] In fact, this was also the common understanding before Lenin.

In Marx's time, most continental European countries had not yet established democratic systems, or if they had, there was no universal suffrage, and the proletariat generally lacked political human rights such as the right to form associations and political parties and vote in elections. I believe it is accurate to call such a representative system "bourgeois democracy" (Marx and Engels never called the later system of universal suffrage bourgeois democracy, as did Lenin). The "democracy" of this time had no way of expressing the will of the poor, and the movements of the lower classes were often violently suppressed. In this context, Marx "say [said] to the workers: You have 15, 20, 50 years of civil war to go through in order to alter the situation and to train yourselves for the exercise of power,"[6] and "the working classes would have to conquer the right to emancipate themselves on the battlefield,"[7] which could lead to the creation of a dictatorship. This idea of fighting violence with violence did indeed have a great impact on later generations.

However, as "bourgeois democracy" made further progress and allowed universal suffrage, the spread of political human rights made it possible for "class competition" to be played out entirely within a constitutional framework, and Engels stopped advocating violent revolution in favor of the constitutional form of leftist movements. Although pure "Gandhism" is rarely accepted, and neither the left nor the right in modern politics has ever guaranteed they would never resort to violence if the rulers were to abolish the constitution and return to tyranny (the United States is now considered a "rightist" state and the citizens' right to bear arms implies that the use of force against tyranny is not excluded), but the violent subversion of constitutional government is unacceptable in modern politics.

At the beginning of the 20th century, only the then still illegal Russian Social Democratic Labor Party, operating in the most authoritarian empire in Europe, referred in its program to the "dictatorship" of the proletariat, a term which was still generally regarded—including by the originator of Russian Marxism, Georgi Plekhanov (1856–1918)—as an option for fighting violence with violence in a state without universal suffrage. But Lenin had another idea. His reason for advocating "dictatorship" was not that the proletariat had to fight violence with violence, but instead that the overwhelming majority of the Russian people were backward peasants, and the proletariat could not win elections, thus it could only seize power violently and use a "dictatorship" to force the backward peasant majority to obey the "advanced minority." In other words, since the "backwardness" of the majority, i.e. the peasants, meant that democracy did not favor the proletariat, the "advanced elements" were forced not only to carry out violent revolution in the face of the repression of the dictatorial tsar, but even after the overthrow of the tsar, they would have to resort to "dictatorship" to overthrow democracy and to force "the 60 peasants to submit to the decisions of the 10 workers."[8] And by the same logic, the ten workers would also obey one or two leaders.

In this way, "dictatorship" ceased to be the wartime state of affairs that it had been from its ancient Roman origins to Marx's era, "a transitory emergency measure, which, so soon as calmer times have set in, will again give place to democracy,"[9] and became a "dictatorship" that extended not only into peacetime, but eventually became an "eternal" posture: "The form of the Soviet Republic as the type of the permanent dictatorship of the proletariat and (in Russia) of the poorer classes of peasants."[10]

What followed is well known: under the name of the "dictatorship of the proletariat," Soviet-style countries never knew what freedom, democracy, constitutionalism, and human rights were. The dictatorship of leaders under the name of one-party rule became the norm. The bloodshed, terror, and death caused by the indiscriminate violence of the state have made people in the modern political civilization blanch at the very idea of "dictatorship." What was meant to be a temporary measure to save democracy in a state of emergency became an even more fearful "totalitarianism."

All of this meant that when a state of emergency was really needed in the West, people were even more hesitant. Which is all the more understandable because the ancient Roman dictator did not in fact return power to the Republic when the emergency was over, but extended the dictatorship into peacetime, a state which extended through the latter era of the Republic, eventually bringing about its fall. The lessons of both ancient and modern times have meant that people are reluctant to lightly explore contingencies, but when something like the Titanic happens, there is no alternative to extraordinary measures. As far as the fight against epidemic disease is concerned, in 1918 the United States employed coercive measures against the "Spanish flu" that would be difficult to implement in the West today. But subsequent human successes against bacterial infections and the democracies' victory over Hitler in World War II, in alliance with the Soviet Union, have greatly increased confidence in democratic governance. The democracies' victory in the Cold War—without the assistance of a totalitarian power, as in World War II—was all the more likely to be seen as the "end of history," marking the triumph of democracy over totalitarianism. In the thirty years that followed, democratic countries have seemed to enjoy a period of prolonged peace for the governments and the people, and when the crisis finally struck they were reluctant to employ emergency measures, and either hesitated repeatedly, thus missing the window of opportunity, or employed light-handed measures, which did not do the job, or revoked the measures too quickly, which made the scourge even worse. There are the bitter lessons to be learned from this fight against the epidemic.

Two Types of Emergencies:
Fighting Epidemics Is Not War

Of course, dictatorships in history, even when they functioned properly, dealt only with states of war. The state of emergency summoned into being by the fight against a severe epidemic is similar to that of wartime, in that they both require necessary and temporary "derogations" from normal human rights to serve vital public interest. But war and epidemics are, after all, emergencies of a different nature. The range of human rights from which they require derogations, and the special mandate/accountability mechanisms are very different. Metaphors such as "winning the war against epidemics" are fine, but epidemic prevention cannot really be considered a war.

The basic difference between fighting epidemics and war is that epidemics are natural disasters, and the germs humans are facing are not a willful enemy, although it is a common metaphor to call a virus an "enemy." In the absence of such an enemy, there is no such thing as winning or losing an epidemic, whereas in war, "victory or defeat is the order of the day."

From the Black Death through the flu, throughout history and all over the world, humankind has experienced many plagues of varying size and severity causing innumerable losses, but as long as the human race has survived without being extermi-nated by the plague, it can be said to have "defeated" it. When there were few casualties in the Haicheng earthquake in 1975, we naturally won, and when we finally achieved a "great victory in our fight against the earthquake disaster" after the Tangshan earthquake in 1976, which in terms of casualties was one of the worst in history, we also "defeated" it.

To put it succinctly, even if it is not a natural disaster but a man-made "germ war" or "virus war," what we would call victory or defeat depends on whether the people of *one side* succumb to the people of *the other side*, and not on whether they succumb to bacteria or viruses. Bacteria and viruses are only a weapon, not a "party to the war." This is like China's battle with the allied forces of England and France in 1860, when the Qing troops suffered heavy casualties from foreign guns and artillery, and the Qing rulers were finally forced to sign the Treaty of Beijing. You can say that the Qing lost to the British and French, but you cannot say they lost to their guns. Decades later in the war against Japan, why were we victorious? Because the Japanese surrendered. Although Chinese civilians and soldiers suffered far more casualties under Japanese attack than during battles with the English and French, victory or defeat always refers to the people who win or lose (British, French, or Japanese), not the weapons employed (whether cold, hot, or biological).

But battles against diseases that are not part of man-made "biological warfare" do not have a winner in this sense. Or, in other words, if the fight against epidemics is likened to a "war," then humankind will always win this war—unless in the future humankind really is exterminated by some disease.

However, although humankind has been the victor in all fights against epidemics throughout history, the success or failure of a particular epidemic has been evaluated very differently. In fact, the only true criterion for this evaluation is the "cost" incurred, which basically refers to the number of human lives lost. Therefore, winning the "war" against an epidemic "at all costs" makes no sense at all if the cost refers to human life. When people go to war, it means that they are willing to pay a certain price, including the sacrifice of human life to achieve a certain result.

Evil wars are often fought without regard for human life, and may even be waged to kill innocent people, as in Hitler's wars to exterminate the Jews. Even in a "just war," the protection of more lives may be one goal among many or the ultimate goal, but there are many "just wars" that are fought for "great causes" other than life, causes such as freedom, dignity, honor, territory, sovereignty, and so forth. This is the origin of lofty expressions such as "give me liberty or give me death."

The achievement of any of these causes requires "victory." Hence, all wars, even just wars, always have victory as the primary objective, and the price of victory is of secondary importance. In order to win, one has to kill (the enemy), and one's own people who are killed in the process are this "price." Even in a just war, "killing 1,000 enemies at the expense of 800" is theoretically acceptable. This is all the more true in practice, and at least in World War II, many countries that resisted German occupation, or China, in its war against Japan—all of which are commonly seen as examples of just wars—military and civilian casualties were far heavier on the righteous side than for the enemy. In the end, however, the righteous side was still victorious.

But the fight against the epidemic is completely different. In the fight against the virus, there is no need to pursue "ultimate victory"—instead, what we should seek is the least cost. Especially in the fight against malignant infectious diseases, can there be any goal other than protecting life? Can the logic of "kill 1,000 enemy soldiers, lose 800 of mine" be applied to the fight against the epidemic? And if we are talking about "losing 800," it is true that we could send one infected person to the incinerator alive and kill the millions of viruses he or she is carrying, but could such an inhumane act be considered fighting the epidemic? No matter how many epidemics there may be, there will always be an end to them, and human beings will not pay reparations and tribute to the virus, let alone sign a treaty of surrender or an "unequal treaty" with the virus. There may be thousands of individual victims in the face of diseases and natural disasters, but humankind will always be the victor. The victor, however, can neither ask for "freedom" from the virus, nor can it obtain reparations and territory. What is the point of humankind's efforts to fight epidemics and disasters if it cannot protect as many individual lives as possible? If "at all costs" means the "cost" of human life, what is the value of winning a "victory" that cannot be lost anyway? Is "minimizing the cost" not the only criterion for evaluating the fight against the epidemic?

Because of the unpredictability of the outcome of a war, those who are granted exceptional wartime powers are usually not subject to exceptional accountability. For example, during wartime in ancient Rome, the dictator had full authority without legal restrictions, and the people did not hold him accountable for his actions during his dictatorship. The only bulwark against his doing bad things was the time limit attached to his mandate: six months or the end of the war, when he had to leave office and hand over power. However, for emergencies such as epidemics or disaster relief, where there is no risk of victory or defeat, the time factor is secondary, and accountability is mandatory. Power can be expanded in a state of emergency, but responsibility must be expanded accordingly. Those who exercise exceptional powers

must be held exceptionally accountable. Correspondingly, those who lose their ordinary rights in a state of emergency should be given extraordinary safeguards. Voluntary medical care for ordinary diseases can be at private expense, but compulsory medical care for those suspected to have virulent infectious diseases must not only be medically accountable, but must also be at public expense (and not only after the infection is confirmed, nor can testing be refused in order to save public funds). Free people can make their own living, but when this right is denied, the government is responsible for the full range of "from cradle to grave" safeguards and must be held fully accountable for them.

In the exercise of power, there is also a difference between war and the fight against epidemics. Soldiers in war must take risks, and sometimes these risks are involuntary, i.e. part of "battlefield discipline." And the "white-coated warriors" on the front lines of the fight against the epidemic deserve the same credit for their dedication and courage as those in the line of fire in war. However, their coercive employment must be clearly distinguished from wartime rules, and so-called "battlefield discipline" must not be imposed lightly. Especially in the prevention and control of highly contagious epidemics, allowing doctors and nurses to carry out the frontline medical work of infectious diseases in the absence of protective gear is not only irresponsible to the lives of medical personnel, but also irresponsible to those receiving care, to the sick, and to society as a whole. This is because frontline health care workers are not only the most vulnerable group, but also the greatest source of infection once they themselves are infected: they work in "congestion" every day,

and this cannot be avoided. Very few of the people they come into contact with in the hospital are indeed suffering from infectious diseases, but the vast majority of them are suffering from various ailments (why else would they be at the hospital) and thus are weak and vulnerable. If the health care workers cannot ensure that they themselves are not infected, then it is not clear whether letting them work is helping or harming people. Finally, if they fall ill, the risk that they will infect others inevitably falls principally on other medical personnel, and at a moment when the epidemic is severe, when medical resources and especially medical personnel are scarce, this is a disaster within a disaster, and is not fighting the epidemic but spreading it.

Unlike soldiers, whose risks affect mainly themselves, the threat of health care workers who become infected goes beyond their own lives. It is therefore not only irresponsible, but downright perverse, for medical personnel to deal with infectious diseases on the front line without protective gear. Because of this practice, the infection rate among medical staff in some places in China was alarmingly high, even much higher than in the people who were coming for treatment: two-thirds of the medical staff in the ICU ward in Wuhan Seventh Hospital were infected. Doctors were severely under-protected, but felt that "they had to go to work even if it was obvious they're going to get sick," which those who were interviewed called "running around naked" practicing medicine. Of the 138 coronavirus patients admitted to Zhongnan Hospital of Wuhan University between January 1 and January 28, fifty-seven were in-hospital infections, forty of which were medical staff, an infection rate of 29%. As many as 262, 194, and

tions on freedom of expression or the suspension of democracy. War, on the other hand, does not require the "confinement" of citizens. A war may result in a ban on strikes or compulsory overtime, but an epidemic may result in a ban on going to work or the imposition of a compulsory "holiday." But for the vast majority of people, lockdowns are worse than restrictions on free speech, and it is conceivable that bans on work are worse than bans on strikes. Here, I would like to highlight the difference in the impact of the two types of state of emergency on freedom of expression.

In wartime emergencies, democratic countries sometimes impose more restrictions on freedom of expression than is usual. There are two reasons for this. The first is to prevent the enemy from deliberately spreading "rumors" and conducting "psychological warfare" to arouse panic, and the second is to prevent unlimited reporting from revealing military secrets to the enemy. However, both of these reasons are based on the existence of a declared enemy and the risk of losing the war. There is no such condition in the fight against the epidemic, and what we call the enemy—the virus—will neither spread malicious rumors nor obtain any secret information our "loose lips" might reveal. As long as it is not the enemy spreading rumors, it is extremely rare in the tradition of freedom of speech for civil discourse to cause panic. The current epidemics in Europe and the United States are proof enough of this: many of these countries have locked down cities for a time to fight epidemics, but they have never denied their people the right to speak, and the result of free speech has not been panic—instead the public's carelessness and excessive "willingness to speak their mind" have been distressing.

This leads us to reflect on the once popular saying in China, "Americans are afraid of death, but Chinese are not." In fact, there are those who are afraid of death and those who are not afraid of death in any country, and those who take chances and those who are really afraid of dying are in the minority, and the general population's tolerance for danger to life is usually somewhere in the middle. But in terms of institutional characteristics, the real difference is that "the American government (i.e., democratic rulers) is afraid of people dying, while the Chinese government (i.e., authoritarian rulers) is not afraid of people dying," at least in wartime, as a comparison of Chinese and American casualties reveals. But the popular saying in China during the pandemic is: "Chinese are obedient, while the Americans are really disobedient; the Chinese are afraid of death, but the Americans are really not afraid of death." If there really is such a thing as "national characteristics," then in the fight against the epidemic, the American character has been very costly in terms of lives lost.[11] This leads one to ask: should the American state interfere with the people's "right to exist" for the sake of their own "survival," and use the power of the state to force them to "fear death?"

In short, the coronavirus pandemic has raised many questions about humankind's political institutions that are well worth pondering. For both China and the West, the questions are both urgent and far-reaching: on the issue of fighting epidemics, China, with its "low human rights advantage," has achieved great success in limiting human rights in order to get the pandemic under control, but it will be a great challenge to prevent the normalization of emergency measures from worsening human rights conditions in normal times. The West, which has actually suffered from the rigidity of its "high human rights" this time around, must learn how a democracy can efficiently enter a state of emergency and how to put an end to emergency measures at the proper time.

In a system that lends itself readily to use of coercive control, in the early stages of the virus, China chose to control the "whistle blowers" and not the virus, and the individuals who are responsible should be punished. In the West however, instead of engaging in political finger-pointing about individual responsibility, they should be reflecting on the shortcomings of the existing democratic system in dealing with emergencies. Democracies may want to review their historical experience of "dictatorship," while China, once the epidemic is over, must work to get rid of "autocracy," "leave the imperial system behind," and practice genuine respect for human rights.

At present, some countries and some politicians are bickering over the responsibility for the global outbreak of the coronavirus epidemic. But in fact, since the virus is not man-made but a natural organism, no one deserves credit or blame for it, no matter where it came from. If it becomes an epidemic, then there is credit and blame to be assigned in terms of whether it is properly handled. Regardless of the origin of the virus, the epidemic started in China, and of course China should bear some moral responsibility to the world for the initial errors in its response that led to the spread of the epidemic. As in the case of the outside world's criticism of China's early mistakes, it is their choice, not their obligation, to praise China's later successes, and China has no "right" to this praise, and the West has the same "right" to selectively study, if they wish, China's later successful experience. For China to thoughtlessly ask the world for thanks is absurd, or at least highly inappropriate. This is like when the white settlers brought smallpox to the New World, causing a catastrophe for the Native Americans, and later the West invented the measures that eradicated smallpox throughout the world. Do the Native Americans "owe the white man a thank you" for that? Could the white man justifiably ask the Native American for such thanks?

But that is not the crux of the issue. What the West should seriously consider is the important flaw in liberal democracy as an institution in the face of the current emergency. Of course you can complain about China's ineffective control in the early stages of the epidemic that led to its spread elsewhere, but when the virus reaches your shores and takes root, and you can't control it with the high level of medical care and the national power at your disposal, does it make sense to blame China? Can blaming China resolve the trade-off between the pros and cons of democracy and authoritarianism in this institutional contest? Imagine again the worst-case scenario: what would you do if democracies and totalitarian states were really engaged in "biological warfare," or "virus warfare"—the deliberate spread of an epidemic to an enemy? If you spread your epidemic in a totalitarian state and they can control it completely with extreme measures, and when they spread theirs in your democracies and you wind up in the same mess you are in today, how can democracy be sustainable? Or does the sustainability of democracy depend on the benevolence of its enemies?

NOTES

Foreword

1   David Ownby, *Reading the China Dream*, https://www.readingthechinadream.com/.

2   See for example, Timothy Cheek, David Ownby, and Joshua A. Fogel, eds., *Voices from the Chinese Century: Public Intellectual Debate from Contemporary China* (New York: Columbia University Press, 2020), and Xu Jilin, *Rethinking China's Rise: A Liberal Critique*, ed. and trans. David Ownby (Cambridge: Cambridge University Press, 2018).

3   David Ownby, "China and the Post-Pandemic World: An Ongoing Project," *Reading the China Dream*, https://www.readingthechinadream.com/china-and-the-post-pandemic-world.html.

4   See, for example, Xu Jilin, "Cultural Factors in Different Models of Fighting the Coronavirus," trans. David Ownby, *Reading the China Dream*, https://www.readingthechinadream.com/xu-jilin-culture-and-coronavirus.html.

5   One of the most interesting is Xiang Biao, "The Theory of 'Concentrated Mobility' and the 'Gyro-Economy:' Understanding Social Change in China through SARS and the Coronavirus," trans. David Ownby, *Reading the China Dream*, https://www.readingthechinadream.com/xiang-biao-concentrated-mobility.html.

6   Details of Qin's biography are drawn, among others, from an interview with Qin entitled "Dividing the Big Family Assets," published in *New Left Review* 20 (March/April 2003), https://newleftreview.org/issues/II20/articles/hui-qin-dividing-the-big-family-assets.

7   The "rustification" of China's urban youth was essentially part of the Cultural Revolution, although similar measures had been employed before. During the Cultural Revolution, urban youth were sent to rural villages or state-run farms beginning in 1968 or 1969, after the initial period of the Cultural Revolution had concluded and central authorities were attempting to reimpose order. Although young people were told that they were to "continue the revolution" and "learn from poor and middle peasants," cynics believe that the idea was motivated more by the need to get unruly young people out of China's cities, where many schools remained closed and the economy was in a shambles, meaning few jobs for high school and university graduates.

8   Qin Hui, *Shichang de zuotian yu jintian: Shangpin jinji, shichang lixing, shehui gongzheng* 市場的昨天與今天：商品經濟、市場理性、社會公正 (Guangzhou: Guangdong Education Publishing House, 1998).

9   Qin Hui, *Gengyun zhe yan: Nongminxue wenji* 耕耘者言：農民學文集 (Guangzhou: Guangdong Education Publishing House, 1999).

10   Qin Hui, *Wenti yu zhuyi* 問題與主義 (Changchun: Changchun Publishing House, 1999).

11   Qin Hui, *Chuantong shi lun: Bentu shehui de zhidu, wenhua ji qi biange* 傳統十論：本土社會的制度、文化及其變革 (Shanghai: Fudan University Press, 2003).

12   Qin Hui, *Nongmin Zhongguo: Lishi fansi yu xianshi xuanzhe* 農民中國：歷史反思與現實選擇 (Zhengzhou: Henan People's Publishing House, 2003).

13   Qin Hui, *Shijian yu ziyou* 實踐與自由 (Hangzhou: Zhejiang People's Publishing House, 2004).

14   Qin Hui, *Biange zhi dao* 變革之道 (Zhengzhou: Zhengzhou University Press, 2007).

15 Qin Hui, *Nanfei de qishi* 南非的啓示 (Nanjing: Jiangsu Phoenix Literature and Art Publishing House, 2013). Part of this work is available online in English translation: Qin Hui, "Looking at China from South Africa," trans. David Ownby, *Reading the China Dream*, https://www.readingthechinadream.com/qin-hui-looking-at-china-from-south-africa.html.

16 Qin Hui, "Dilemmas of Twenty-First Century Globalization: Explanations and Solutions, with a Critique of Thomas Piketty's *Twenty-First Century Capitalism*," trans. David Ownby, *Reading the China Dream*, https://www.readingthechinadream.com/qin-hui-dilemmas.html.

17 Qin Hui, *Zouchu dizhi* 走出帝制 (Beijing: Qunyan Press, 2015).

18 "*Qin Hui: Minzhu renquan, qun ji quanjie yu jinji zhuangtai: quanqiu yiqingxia de fansi*" 秦輝：民主人權、群己權界與緊急狀態：全球疫情下的反思, YouTube, April 30, 2020, https://www.youtube.com/watch?v=r7CgHyeeqlA.

Chapter One

* The title of Chapter One is a virtually untranslatable, bilingual pun: "*'Ren zuo' huo 'ren you' de kunhuo*"「人左」或「人右」的困惑. 人左 means literally "people left," 人右 "people right," and 困惑 "riddle" or "puzzle." Neither "people left" nor "people right" has any meaning in Chinese, and it is only after reading further in the text that one realizes he means "people on the left," i.e., those who wear a mask, and "people on the right," those who insist on their rights, which leads to the play of words, in English, opposing "human rights" with no humans "left." — Trans.

1 Jay O'Brien and William Roseberry, *Golden Ages, Dark Ages: Imagining the Past in Anthropology and History* (University of California Press, 1991), 25.

2 John Munro, "Before and After the Black Death: Money, Prices, and Wages in Fourteenth-Century England" (working paper, Department

sent abroad by the state, because the students paying their own way had themselves decided to leave. This logic goes completely against common sense: should not those who are sent abroad by the state be all the more obedient to the orders of that state, and assume risks for their fellow citizens? Why is it that they should have their way paid when they go abroad and have special privileges when they come back? Actually I approve of the idea of preventing the return of Chinese who are in countries affected by the pandemic, but we should thank them for understanding China's current difficulties and for sacrificing their rights and facing security risks and economic burdens, not slander them without mercy.

20 *"Yao Yang: Zhongguo de diyinsi baohu zhuangtai gei AI fazhan tigongle youshi"* 姚洋：中國的低隱私保護狀態給 AI 發展提供了優勢, Caixin.com, November 11, 2019, http://video.caixin.com/2019-11-09/101481276. html.

21 Of course, it seems that there is also a fourth way, which is to ignore it, on the premise that the death rate is not high, and after more people come down with the disease, those who do not die will be immune, which is called "herd immunity." But is this not what people — and even apes — did before the development of civilization? So in fact, this is the "method" you use when you have no method, and I will not include it.

22 North Korea might be an exception. I have heard that the North Korean government has a harsh policy of executing all suspected infected persons and burning their corpses, so there have been no serious outbreaks in the country that lies between two major sources of the epidemic, China and South Korea.

23 Christine M. Boeckl, *Images of Plague and Pestilence: Iconography and Iconology* (Kirksville, Missouri: Truman State University Press, 2000), 15, 27.

24 Edward Livingston Youmans, *Class-Book of Chemistry* (New York: D. Appleton & Co., 1858), https://commons.wikimedia.org/wiki/File:John_Stenhouse%27s_mask.png.

25   In the official photo of Wu Liande being received by the regent in China, Wu wore a German-style military uniform, a style which was neither that of the Qing nor the later ROC style, which was a special favor extended by the Qing court to "foreign officers."

26   Martin C. J. Bootsma and Neil M. Ferguson, "The Effect of Public Health Measures on the 1918 Influenza Pandemic in US cities," *Proceedings of the National Academy of Sciences* 104, no. 18 (2007): 7588–7593.

27   *Ch'eng-tan* 城旦 refers to the prisoners who were being forced to build the city walls. ——Ed.

28   A. F. P. Hulsewé, *Remnants of Ch'in Law: An Annotated Translation of the Ch'in Legal and Administrative Rules of the 3rd Century BC* (Leiden: Brill, 1985), 155.

29   Eugenia Tognotti, "Lessons from the History of Quarantine, from Plague to Influenza A," *Emerging Infectious Diseases* 19, no. 2 (2013): 254–259.

30   Chen's story is told on the American podcast *This American Life*. See Jiayang Fan, "Mr. Chen Goes to Wuhan," *This American Life*, https://www.thisamericanlife.org/695/everyones-a-critic/act-two-19. ——Trans.

31   Of course, when the epidemic is so severe that medical resources are depleted, it is not practical to carry out isolation for all patients. However, this is not controversial. At the beginning of Wuhan's closure, there were also many patients who could not be seen, could not be tested and diagnosed, could not be admitted after diagnosis and had to be "isolated at home," and even died at home without being admitted, diagnosed or even seen. Later on, the number of confirmed diagnoses increased several times and the number of deaths increased by as much as 50% due to this situation. This kind of helplessness is of course no kind of "achievement" at all.

32   Philip A. Mackowiak and Paul S. Sehdev, "The Origin of Quarantine." *Clinical Infectious Diseases*, 35, no. 9 (2002): 1071–1072. Another way of looking at the history of medicine is that the quarantine system began

in Venice: "In 1348, Venice establishes the world's first institutionalized quarantine system, giving a council of three the power to detain their ships, goods, and individuals in the Venetian lagoon for up to 40 days." Peter Tyson, "A Short History of Quarantine", Public Broadcasting Service, October 11, 2004, https://www.pbs.org/wgbh/nova/article/short-history-of-quarantine/.

33   Gian Franco Gensini, Magdi H. Yacouba and Andrea A. Conti, "The Concept of Quarantine in History: From Plague to SARS," *Journal of Infection* 49, no. 4 (2004): 257–261.

34   Luke 16: 26 (New International Version).

35   Laura H. Rosenberger et al., "Quarantine, Isolation, and Cohorting: From Cholera to *Klebsiella*," *Surgical Infections* 13, no. 2 (2012): 69–73.

36   Peter Tyson, "A Short History of Quarantine".

Chapter Two

1   Eugenia Tognotti, "Lessons from the History of Quarantine, from Plague to Influenza A," 256–258.

2   Ibid.

3   Many studies have pointed out that many people who are traditionally isolated as lepers actually had syphilis or other diseases.

4   "Koizumi Apologises for Leper Colonies," *BBC World News,* May 25, 2001, http://news.bbc.co.uk/2/hi/asia-pacific/1350630.stm.

5   "Japan's Leprosy Policy Denounced," *BBC World News*, March 2, 2005, http://news.bbc.co.uk/2/hi/asia-pacific/4311679.stm.

6   *Encyclopedia Britannica*, 11th ed. (1911), s.v. "quarantine."

7   "About Quarantine and Isolation," Centers for Disease Control and Prevention, https://www.cdc.gov/quarantine/quarantineisolation.html.

8   Tognotti, "Lessons from the History of Quarantine, from Plague to Influenza A," 257–259.

9   Ibid.

10   Eugenia Tognotti, "I'm a Historian of Epidemics and Quarantine. Now

I'm Living That History on Lockdown in Italy," *Time*, March 11, 2020, https://time.com/5800993/quarantine-historian-italy/.

11   Ibid.

12   A PDF of this document may be found here: https://www.refworld.org/docid/4672bc122.html.

13   Pabst Battin, Leslie P. Francis and Jay A. Jacobson, *The Patient as Victim and Vector: Ethics and Infectious Disease* (Oxford: Oxford University Press, 2009).

14   Tognotti, "Lessons from the History of Quarantine, from Plague to Influenza A," 258–259.

15   K. W. Todrys, E. Howe and J. J. Amoncor, "Failing Siracusa: Governments' Obligations to Find the Least Restrictive Options for Tuberculosis Control," *Public Health Action,* 3 no. 1 (2013): 7–10.

16   David Ross, *The Right and the Good* (Oxford: Clarendon Press, 1930).

17   Qin is referring here to one of the key arguments advanced by the Chinese state for why Western-style democracy is not appropriate for China: China is still a developing country, which suggests that a right to "subsistence" is more important than, for example, the right to vote. The point is argued in one of China's early "White Papers" in the early 1990s and is still evoked today, despite China's considerable progress. —Trans.

18   "*Qin Hui, Xu Zhangrun, Wang Yiwei, Wang Wen: Jibian renquan yu zhuquan*" 秦輝、許章潤、王義桅、王文：激辯人權與主權, Legal-Theory, December 30, 2014, https://www.legal-theory.org/?mod=info&act=view&id=20562.

19   This has to do with the Anlu Shan rebellion (755–763), a major uprising during the Tang period. Yang Guifei, and indeed her entire family, had been close to Anlu Shan, who had been part of the imperial entourage before leading the uprising, and the Yangs thus took some of the blame for the events. The reference to Maweipo refers to a place in which the emperor and the court took refuge when they were forced to flee the capital. There was a near mutiny, with several of the emperors' generals demanding the death of the Yang clan, and the emperor acquiesced despite his love for Yang Guifei. —Trans.

20 Liu Shaoqi (1898–1969) was a high-ranking member of the CCP and Mao's right-hand man on various occasions, but became the object of attacks on "revisionists" during the Cultural Revolution. Liu died while in captivity, reportedly from being denied the insulin he needed as a diabetic. —Trans.

21 Lin Zhao (1932–1968) joined the CCP as a teenager, but eventually became a dissident and dared to criticize Chairman Mao. She was executed in 1968. —Trans.

22 *"Qin Hui, Xu Zhangrun, Wang Yiwei, and Wang Wen: Jibian renquan yu zhuquan"* 秦輝、許章潤、王義桅、王文：激辯人權與主權.

23 Many people identity such demands with what Isaiah Berlin called "positive freedom." In fact, Berlin's positive freedom meant something else, but positive rights do indeed exist.

24 Karl Marx, "Chapter Twenty-Eight: Bloody Legislation against the Expropriated, from the End of the 15th Century. Forcing down of Wages by Acts of Parliament," *Capital*, Volume 1, https://www.marxists.org/archive/marx/works/1867-c1/ch28.htm.

Chapter Three

1 Qin's reference is to the story of the "three monks." At the beginning of the story, one monk lived alone in a temple at the top of a hill, and, using a shoulder pole, brought up two buckets of water every day. A second monk arrived, and they tried to cooperate by sharing their labor, but the pole was too short for use by two people and they could only carry one bucket of water, much of which splashed out as they climbed the hill. Finally, a third monk arrived, who simply drank the water. The two original monks forced the newly arrived monk to haul up two buckets of water, which he did, but then he drank them both. Everyone went on strike until a fire in the temple made them realize that cooperation was the only solution, and they devised a pulley system to bring water to the hilltop. —Trans.

2   Qin Hui, *Gongtong de dixian* 共同的底綫 (Nanjing: Jiangsu Phoenix Art Publishing House, 2013).

3   Robespierre stated in December 1793 that "The object of a revolutionary regime is to found a republic; that of a constitutional regime is to carry it on. The first befits a time of war between liberty and its enemies; the second suits a time when freedom is victorious, and at peace with the world." Translation taken from John Kekes, "Why Robespierre Chose Terror: The lessons of the First Totalitarian Revolution," *City Journal* (Spring 2006), https://www.city-journal.org/html/why-robespierre-chose-terror-12935.html.

4   Vladimir Lenin, "The Proletarian Revolution and the Renegade Kautsky," in *Lenin Collected Works,* Volume 28 (July 1918–March 1919), ed. Jim Riordan (Moscow: Progress Publishers, 1965), 236.

5   Roy Medvedev, *Leninism and Western Socialism* (London: Verso Books, 1981), 36.

6   "Meeting of the Central Authority, September 15, 1850," in Karl Marx and Frederick Engels, *Marx & Engels Collected Works*, Volume 10 (1849–1851) (London: Lawrence & Wishart, 1978), 628.

7   "Record of Marx's Speech on the Seventh Anniversary of the International," in Karl Marx and Frederick Engels, *Marx & Engels Collected Works*, Volume 22 (1870–1871) (London: Lawrence & Wishart, 1986), 634.

8   Vladimir Lenin, "First All-Russia Congress on Adult Education," in *Lenin Collected Works,* Volume 29 (March–August 1919), ed. George Hanna (Moscow: Progress Publishers, 1965), 367.

9   Karl Kautsky, *The Dictatorship of the Proletariat,* trans. H. J. Stenning (London and Leicester: National Labour Press, 1919), 141.

10 Ibid, 142.

11 Some people argue that the total death rate in the United States during the epidemic fell rather than rose due to a reduction in car accidents, but this is absurd. Similarly, a higher death rate from car accidents is not a reason to ignore the number of violent deaths involving weapons.

Battin, Pabst, Leslie P. Francis, and Jay A. Jacobson. *The Patient as Victim and Vector: Ethics and Infectious Disease*. Oxford: Oxford University Press, 2009.

Boeckl, Christine M. *Images of Plague and Pestilence: Iconography and Iconology*. Kirksville, Missouri: Truman State University Press, 2000.

Bootsma, Martin C. J., and Neil M. Ferguson. "The Effect of Public Health Measures on the 1918 Influenza Pandemic in US Cities." *Proceedings of the National Academy of Sciences* 104, no. 18 (2007): 7588–7593.

Centers for Disease Control and Prevention. "About Quarantine and Isolation." https://www.cdc.gov/quarantine/quarantineisolation.html.

Cheek, Timothy, David Ownby, and Joshua A. Fogel. *Voices from the Chinese Century: Public Intellectual Debate from Contemporary China*. New York: Columbia University Press, 2020.

Domar, Evsey D. "The Causes of Slavery or Serfdom: A Hypothesis." *The Journal of Economic History* 30, no. 1 (1970): 18–32.

Fan, Jiayang. "Mr. Chen Goes to Wuhan." *This American Life*, https://www.thisamericanlife.org/695/everyones-a-critic/act-two-19.

Gensini, Gian Franco, Magdi H. Yacouba, and Andrea A. Conti, "The Concept of Quarantine in History: From Plague to SARS." *Journal of Infection* 49, no. 4 (2004): 257–261.

Hua Sheng. *Hua Sheng 2010* (blog), Weibo, https://www.weibo.com/u/1223237202.

Hulsewe, A. F. P. *Remnants of Ch'in Law: An Annotated Translation of the Ch'in Legal and Administrative Rules of the 3rd Century BC*. Leiden: Brill, 1985.

Kautsky, Karl. *The Dictatorship of the Proletariat*. Translated by H. J. Stenning. London and Leicester: National Labour Press, 1919.

Kekes, John. "Why Robespierre Chose Terror: The lessons of the First Totalitarian Revolution." *City Journal* (Spring 2006). https://www.city-journal.org/html/why-robespierre-chose-terror-12935.html.

Lenin, Vladimir. "First All-Russia Congress on Adult Education." In *Lenin Collected Works,* Volume 29 (March–August 1919), edited by George Hanna, 367. Moscow: Progress Publishers, 1965.

———. "The Proletarian Revolution and the Renegade Kautsky." In *Lenin Collected Works,* Volume 28 (July 1918–March 1919), edited by Jim Riordan, 236. Moscow: Progress Publishers, 1965.

Mackowiak, Philip A., and Paul S. Sehdev, "The Origin of Quarantine." *Clinical Infectious Diseases, 35*, no. 9 (2002): 1071–1072.

Marx, Karl. "Chapter Twenty-Eight: Bloody Legislation against the Expropriated, from the End of the 15th Century. Forcing down of Wages by Acts of Parliament." In *Capital*, Volume 1. Moscow: Progress Publishers, 1887. https://www.marxists.org/archive/marx/works/1867-c1/ch28.htm.

Medvedev, Roy. *Leninism and Western Socialism*. London: Verso Books, 1981.

Munro, John. "Before and After the Black Death: Money, Prices, and Wages in Fourteenth-Century England." Working paper, Department of Economics and Institute for Policy Analysis, University of Toronto, Toronto, 2004. https://www.economics.utoronto.ca/public/working-Papers/UT-ECIPA-MUNRO-04-04.pdf.

O'Brien, Jay, and William Roseberry. *Golden Ages, Dark Ages: Imagining the Past in Anthropology and History*. Berkely: University of California Press, 1991.

Ownby, David. "China and the Post-Pandemic World: An Ongoing Project,"

Reading the China Dream, https://www.readingthechinadream.com/china-and-the-post-pandemic-world.html.

———. *Reading the China Dream*, https://www.readingthechinadream.com/.

Peters, Maggie. "Labor Markets after the Black Death: Landlord Collusion and the Imposition of Serfdom in Eastern Europe and the Middle East." Stanford Department of Political Science, January 10, 2011. https://politicalscience.stanford.edu/events/comparative-politics-workshop/labor-markets-after-black-death-landlord-collusion-and.

Qin, Hui. "Dilemmas of Twenty-First Century Globalization: Explanations and Solutions, with a Critique of Thomas Piketty's Twenty-First Century Capitalism." Translated by David Ownby, *Reading the China Dream*, https://www.readingthechinadream.com/qin-hui-dilemmas.html.

———. "Looking at China from South Africa." Translated by David Ownby, *Reading the China Dream*, https://www.readingthechinadream.com/qin-hui-looking-at-china-from-south-africa.html.

———. *Biange zhi dao* 變革之道. Zhengzhou: Zhengzhou University Press, 2007.

———. *Chuantong shi lun: Bentu shejui de zhidu, wenhua ji qi biange* 傳統十論：本土社會的制度、文化及其變革. Shanghai: Fudan University Press, 2003.

———. *Gengyun zhe yan: Nongminxue wenji* 耕耘者言：農民學文集. Guangzhou: Guangdong Education Publishing House, 1999.

———. *Gongtong de dixian* 共同的底綫. Nanjing: Jiangsu Phoenix Art Publishing House, 2013.

———. *Nanfei de qishi* 南非的啓示. Nanjing: Jiangsu Phoenix Literature and Art Publishing House, 2013.

———. *Nongmin Zhongguo: Lishi fansi yu xianshi xuanzhe* 農民中國：歷史反思與現實選擇. Zhengzhou: Henan People's Publishing House, 2003.

———. *Shichang de zuotian yu jintian: Shangpin jinji, shichang lixing, shehui gongzheng* 市場的昨天與今天：商品經濟、市場理性、社會公正. Guangzhou: Guangdong Education Publishing House, 1998.

————. *Shijian yu ziyou* 實踐與自由. Hangzhou: Zhejiang People's Publishing House, 2004.

————. *Wenti yu zhuyi* 問題與主義. Changchun: Changchun Publishing House, 1999.

————. *Zouchu dizhi* 走出帝制. Beijing: Qunyan Press, 2015.

Rosenberger, Laura H., et al., "Quarantine, Isolation, and Cohorting: From Cholera to *Klebsiella*." *Surgical Infections* 13, no. 2 (2012): 69–73.

Ross, David. *The Right and the Good*. Oxford: Clarendon Press, 1930.

Tianlinxian zhi 田林縣志 (Tianlin County Annals). Nanning: Guangxi People's Publishing House, 1996.

Todrys, K. W., E. Howe, and J. J. Amoncor. "Failing Siracusa: Governments' Obligations to Find the Least Restrictive Options for Tuberculosis Control." *Public Health Action,* 3 no. 1 (2013): 7–10.

Tognotti, Eugenia. "I'm a Historian of Epidemics and Quarantine. Now I'm Living That History on Lockdown in Italy." *Time*, March 11, 2020, https://time.com/5800993/quarantine-historian-italy/.

————. "Lessons from the History of Quarantine, from Plague to Influenza A." *Emerging Infectious Diseases* 19, no. 2 (2013): 254–259.

Tyson, Peter. "A Short History of Quarantine." *Public Broadcasting Service*, October 11, 2004, https://www.pbs.org/wgbh/nova/article/short-history-of-quarantine/.

Xiang, Biao. "The Theory of 'Concentrated Mobility' and the 'Gyro-Economy:' Understanding Social Change in China through SARS and the Coronavirus." Translated by David Ownby, *Reading the China Dream*, https://www.readingthechinadream.com/xiang-biao-concentrated-mobility.html.

Xu, Jilin. "Cultural Factors in Different Models of Fighting the Coronavirus." Translated by David Ownby, *Reading the China Dream*, https://www.readingthechinadream.com/xu-jilin-culture-and-coronavirus.html.

————. *Rethinking China's Rise: A Liberal Critique*. Edited and translated by David Ownby. Cambridge: Cambridge University Press, 2018.

Youmans, Edward Livingston. *Class-Book of Chemistry*. New York: D. Appleton & Co., 1858.

"Dividing the Big Family Assets." *New Left Review* 20 (March/April 2003), https://newleftreview.org/issues/II20/articles/hui-qin-dividing-the-big-family-assets.

"Japan's Leprosy Policy Denounced." *BBC World News*, March 2, 2005, http://news.bbc.co.uk/2/hi/asia-pacific/4311679.stm.

"Koizumi Apologises for Leper Colonies." *BBC World News*, May 25, 2001, http://news.bbc.co.uk/2/hi/asia-pacific/1350630.stm.

"Meeting of the Central Authority, September 15, 1850." In Karl Marx and Frederick Engels, *Marx & Engels Collected Works*, Volume 10 (1849–1851), 625–629. London: Lawrence & Wishart, 1978.

"*Qin Hui, Xu Zhangrun, Wang Yiwei, Wang Wen: Jibian renquan yu zhuquan*" 秦輝、許章潤、王義桅、王文：激辯人權與主權. *LegalTheory*, December 30, 2014, https://www.legaltheory.org/?mod=info&act=view&id=20562.

"*Qin Hui: Minzhu renquan, qun ji quanjie yu jinji zhuangtai: Quanqiu yiqing xia de fansi*" 秦輝：民主人權、群己權界與緊急狀態：全球疫情下的反思. YouTube, April 30, 2020, https://www.youtube.com/watch?v=r7C-gHyeeqlA.

"Record of Marx's Speech on the Seventh Anniversary of the International." In Karl Marx and Frederick Engels, *Marx & Engels Collected Works*, Volume 22 (1870–1871), 633–634. London: Lawrence & Wishart, 1986.

"*Weiwen daojia 'Gongan ruhu bashou' dou shi jiade bu rang hanle*" 維穩到家「公安入戶把守」都是假的，不讓喊了. *China Digital Times*, March 10, 2020, https://chinadigitaltimes.net/chinese/637823.html.

"*Yao Yang: Zhongguo de diyinsi baohu zhuangtai gei AI fazhan tigongle youshi*" 姚洋：中國的低隱私保護狀態給AI發展提供了優勢. Caixin Video & Audio, November 11, 2019, http://video.caixin.com/2019-11-09/101481276.html.

"*Zuikuihoushou jiu shi Hubei Wuhan zhushiren! Zhiming jingjixuejia shimingzhikong*" 罪魁禍首就是湖北武漢主事人！知名經濟學家實名指控. Zhihu, March 4, 2020, https://zhuanlan.zhihu.com/p/110821445.